8-95

CW00557046

SUPERVISION

SAGE HUMAN SERVICES GUIDES, VOLUME 35

SAGE HUMAN SERVICES GUIDES

a series of books edited by ARMAND LAUFFER and CHARLES D. GARVIN. Published in cooperation with the University of Michigan School of Social Work and other organizations.

(S) A **SAGE** HUMAN SERVICES GUIDE **35**

SUPERVISION
A Decision–Making Approach

Eileen GAMBRILL
Theodore J. STEIN

Published in cooperation with the University of Michigan School of Social Work

(S) **SAGE** PUBLICATIONS
The Publishers of Professional Social Science
Newbury Park   London   New Delhi

For information address:

SAGE Publications, Inc.
2111 West Hillcrest Drive
Newbury Park, California 91320

SAGE Publications Ltd.
28 Banner Street
London EC1Y 8QE
England

SAGE Publications India Pvt. Ltd.
M-32 Market
Greater Kailash I
New Delhi 110 048 India

Printed in the United States of America
Library of Congress Cataloging in Publication Data

Gambrill, Eileen.
    Supervision: a decision-making approach.

    (Sage human services guides ; 35)
    "Published in cooperation with the University of Michigan School of Social Work."
    Bibliography: p.
    Includes index.
    1. Social work administration—United States. 2. Decision-making. 3. Social case work. I. Stein, Theodore J. II. Title. III. Series: Sage human services guides; v. 35.
HV95.G33   1983   361.3'068   83-17727

THIRD PRINTING, 1989

CONTENTS

PREFACE

The purpose of this book is to add to your repertoire of supervisory skills. Supervision is viewed here within a decision-making framework, in recognition of the many decisions supervisors have to make and help others make. In spite of the considerable challenge involved in being an effective supervisor, often little training is provided to assume this important position. Recognition of this lack has resulted in increased attention to the supervisory role over the past few years. We define effective supervisors as those who help their staff help their clients in a manner that maximizes positive consequences for all.

This book grew out of our earlier efforts to design a procedure that would help child welfare workers make timely decisions concerning children and their families (see Stein et al., 1978). It was obvious that a training program for supervisors was necessary to complement material developed for line staff (Gambrill and Stein, 1978). Generic features of the decision-making procedure developed are highlighted in this book. We are grateful to the Department of Health, Education and Welfare, San Francisco, California, for awarding us a training grant for development and diffusion of training materials for supervisors. The positive feedback we received from supervisors encouraged us to make this material more widely available.

This book is organized in terms of key decisions that you have to make in your role as a supervisor. Research supporting the need for a systematic decision-making procedure is briefly discussed in Chapter 1. The role of supervision in social work and sources of our information are also briefly described in this chapter. You must make decisions concerning the quality of intake services and the extent to which such services meet agency requirements. Chapter 2 describes a framework for making intake decisions. You must decide how to balance caseloads, how to assign priorities, and how to keep track of plans made for clients. Knowledge of plans workers make for clients is important in determining workload, since some plans require more time and effort than others. Also, some plans are more desirable than others. For example, if agency policy states that people should not be removed from their homes unless this is absolutely necessary, one of your tasks will be to make sure that this policy is followed. If a worker plans to move an unusually high number of elderly clients into out-of-home placement, you should examine whether such a plan is best for all these clients. Chapter 3 describes a procedure for keeping track of all cases in a unit in terms of plans made and procedures used to follow these through to completion.

Subsequent chapters describe decision-making guidelines in relation to other important supervisory tasks, including reviewing the quality of assessment (Chapter 4); intervention and evaluation (Chapter 5); and coordination of services (Chapter 6). Methods to encourage effective staff behavior are described in Chapter 7. Other topics discussed include guidelines for selecting training programs (Chapter 8); important interpersonal competencies (Chapter 9); and maintaining effective supervisory skills (Chapter 10).

Administrative, educational, and supportive components of supervision are often treated as separate when, in fact, they are closely related. Examples are offered in this book of the interconnections among these three components. For example, evaluation of your staff's success in achieving outcomes desired by clients fulfills an important administrative function. This also offers information about training needs and opportunities to provide positive feedback to your staff. We have highlighted the importance of positive monitoring (attending to achievements and assets) rather than negative monitoring (attending to mistakes and deficiencies).

We would like to offer a special acknowledgement to Vivian Sutcher, University Extension, University of California, Berkeley for her support and excellent help and suggestions in preparing the training grant and carrying out training programs. We thank the many supervisors in many different states who participated in training programs and who offered valuable feedback. Comments from supervisors who were not in child welfare about the usefulness of the material encouraged us to identify generic features in the methods described. We are grateful to Professor Armand Lauffer for encouraging us to pursue this task and for his very helpful suggestions. Finally, we offer a special note of appreciation to Professor Emeritus Kermit Wiltse of the University of California at Berkeley for encouraging our interest in the field of child welfare.

Chapter 1

INTRODUCTION

Offering high quality services to clients is an interest shared by all social workers. As resources shrink, achieving this outcome becomes even more of a challenge. This book describes decision-making procedures that you can use to increase the likelihood that clients will receive effective services. Supervisors occupy a key role in assuring that effective services are offered to clients. They are responsible for administrative, educational, and supportive tasks. They are in close contact with line staff and hence can monitor the quality of their work. Supervisors are in the best position to see that accurate data are gathered that will be of value to higher-level administration. They are often responsible for communicating agency policy to workers, as well as for staff development. Increased burdens have been placed on supervisors because of moratoriums on hiring and the hiring of untrained workers in positions previously held by trained staff. These difficulties are compounded by the trend of moving workers with no specialized training or experience in one area, such as child welfare, into positions once held by trained staff. There is increased emphasis on accountability. Supervisors must monitor the quality of services provided and offer positive incentives for effective performance if high-quality services are to be offered to clients. How can this be done given the task involved? Each supervisor may be responsible for seven workers, each of whom carries a minimum of 40 cases. The methods described in this book should make this task easier to accomplish.

Offering effective service is viewed here within a decision-making framework. The daily tasks of social workers require continual decision making in terms of who is eligible for services, what services should be provided, what goals and objectives should be selected, what assessment information should be gathered, what intervention procedures should be used, and how progress should be evaluated. Every day you make scores of decisions that influence the quality of services offered to clients. These include decisions about priorities for service delivery,

intake, the quality of assessment, intervention, and evaluation procedures used by staff, the utility of record-keeping procedures, feedback to
offer your staff, how to encourage more effective staff performance,
what training materials to offer, how to cope with being supervised,
how to maintain effective supervisory behaviors, and how to avoid or
resolve interpersonal dilemmas. Guidelines for making these decisions
are described in this book. Before moving on to these topics it will be
helpful to take a brief look at the role of supervision within social work.
Value assumptions and sources of information drawn upon in design of
our decision-making framework are also discussed.

PRACTICE TASK 1.1

Write down two decisions you find easy to make in your role as a
supervisor. What is it about these two decisions that make them easy
to make?

PRACTICE TASK 1.2

Write down two decisions that are difficult for you to make. What
would make it easier to arrive at these decisions?

THE ROLE OF SUPERVISION
IN SOCIAL WORK

Kadushin (1976) has presented a historical perspective on the use of
supervision in social work practice and discusses why it has assumed a
role of such importance in this field, compared with other professions.
He mentions a number of factors that may account for this:

(1) Services are provided through an agency that requires a
    bureaucratic structure to operate well. The work of many
    people must be coordinated.
(2) The activity of social workers involves the distribution of
    services that are not owned by the agency, and the community
    that funds these resources exerts pressure for accountability.
(3) Agency policies often originate from political groups, to which
    the agency is responsible both for the management of funds
    and the resolution of important social problems.

(4) The autonomy granted by the community to social workers is constrained by the lack of clarity concerning the objectives of social work and disagreement concerning goals.

(5) "Where objectives are unclear, where there is great uncertainty as to how to proceed, where the effects of intervention are unpredictable and the risk of failure is high, workers may need and want the availability of an administrative representative with whom they can share responsibility for decision making, from whom they receive direction, and to whom they can look for support" (1976: 27).

(6) The practice of social workers is usually not directly observed. Thus supervision is critical in order to protect clients from harmful practice.

(7) The relation between social work services and outcome is often hard to define objectively.

(8) Clients are often "captives" (p. 28) of the agency, thus entailing a greater need to protect clients. (In child welfare, natural parents are often captives of the court.)

(9) Many social workers have a tenuous commitment to social work, which leads to a high turnover rate and thus to a recurrent need to train new workers; thus supervisors serve an important socialization and administrative function.

(10) Social work lacks effective professional or organizational controls.

(11) Many social workers have limited training. Also, they operate on limited shared knowledge, and consequently want to share decisional responsibilities.

(12) The problems encountered in social work, such as illness, dependency, and the risk of failure, make heavy emotional demands. "There are few professions that come close to social work in developing in the worker the need for support, encouragement, reassurance, and restoration of morale — a need met by supportive supervision" (p. 35).

(13) There is a lack of opposition to the development of a supervisory process that Kadushin feels has been and still is facilitated by the high percentage of women in social work and by the characteristics of those who enter social work. For example, Gockel (1967) found that undergraduate students who specialized in social work were less likely to express a desire for freedom from supervision, compared to students who remained outside of the field.

Nothing can be done to alter some of the factors mentioned. Services are located within a bureaucratic structure; resources are not owned by the agency; policies are influenced by groups external to the agency; and the problems clients bring to social workers and the decisions required are difficult. However, you can do something about many other factors. Objectives, goals, and progress indicators can be clearly described, as well as assessment and intervention procedures, allowing more accurate assessment of services provided and progress achieved. Available knowledge about helpful procedures can be used. Your role will be more difficult to the extent to which the factors mentioned by Kadushin (1976) are operative. If objectives are unclear, if priorities are not established, if assessment and intervention procedures are not clearly described, if progress indicators are vague, then all aspects of supervision, including the administrative, educational, and supportive components, will be difficult.

PRACTICE TASK 1.3

Are there characteristics of your agency that make decision making especially difficult? If so, what are some of these?

Are there any characteristics of your agency that make decision making especially easy in your agency? If so, what are these?

THE NEED FOR A DECISION-MAKING FRAMEWORK

The decisions social workers make are weighty. Their consequences are often severe and may result in denial of services, removal of clients from one environment to another, and termination of certain rights. Despite the importance of decision making at all stages of the case process, only in recent years have procedural guidelines been developed to assist workers in making choices. A series of decisions are common to cases served in all social work settings. For example, workers must decide whether applicants are eligible for service, whether to provide services in the home or in some other setting, what services are most likely to reduce or eliminate presenting problems, and who should provide these services. Criteria should be described for making each decision and rules established for using information. The end product of identifying decisions and related criteria and rules is a framework for making decisions in a service area.

Decision making involves four steps. First, possible alternatives must be identified. Second, information is gathered using criteria that permit sorting of material into categories of relevant and irrelevant data. Next, rules are used to weigh data in terms of importance for making required decisions. Use of these rules may be sufficient to reach a decision. For example, the decision to move a client into community-based work can easily be made if a job is available and the client has required skills. When criteria and rules are not sufficient to reach a decision, judgment must be exercised in the selection of options. The importance of having criteria for decision making and rules for using information has long been recognized. Without these, workers may gather excessive amounts of information (Stein, 1974, 1982; Golan, 1969; Brieland, 1959) and personal values, biases, and attitudes will influence choices made (Emlen et al., 1976, 1977). Workers' attitudes, often unsupported by facts, profoundly influence worker behavior (Emlen et al., 1976, 1977). Social workers often focus on the pathology of clients rather than client assets and resources. Emlen et al. (1977) noted that conditions diagnosed as irremediable were often found to be in error and that clients responded to proper evaluation and treatment. They found that the general climate of attitudes in the particular county where the worker practiced strongly influenced the worker's planning decisions (1977: 43).

Efforts to develop a framework for decision making based on empirical investigations have often produced disappointing results. For example, efforts have been made to identify factors that influence decisions made at child welfare intake. Neither Mech (1970) nor Runyan (1982) found any factors that differentiated between children placed in foster care and those maintained in their own homes. Although some reports found that a worker's evaluation of maternal care was a prime factor in decisions to place children (Boehm, 1962, Shinn, 1969), others found no evidence that maternal functioning was relevant to such decisions (Phillips et al., 1971). Some writers suggest that the availability of resources influences a worker's decisions (Shyne, 1969; Jenkins and Sauber, 1966) and that placement of children could be avoided if day-care and homemaker services were available (Jenkins and Sauber, 1966). Other investigators have found no association between availability of resources and placement decisions (Gruber, 1978; Stein, 1974; Rapp, 1982).

Phillips et al. (1971) compared intake decisions of social workers from three agencies with those of independent judges, each of whom had more than five years of experience in child welfare. "The judges agreed with each other and with the workers on less than one-half of the cases; when they did agree they did not identify the same factors" (1971: 84). Wolins (1963) found that agreement between worker-judges, basing their decision on material in the case record, was poor. However, agreement increased when workers received only information considered most relevant to the decision. Stein and Rzepnicki (forthcoming) found a high degree of agreement between judges for decisions made at child welfare intake when specific criteria and rules for using information were used in reviewing case records.

SOURCES OF INFORMATION ABOUT DECISION MAKING

Decision making should be guided by knowledge of predictable outcomes. Each time, for example, that a client is removed from his or her home, a decision is made that this person will be better off in another setting. Few variables on which information is available have much predictive utility. However, decision making should be guided by what information *is* available. For example, we know that parental visiting of their children who are in out-of-home care is related to outcome (e.g. Fanshel and Shinn, 1978). Willingness to sign a service contract is predictive of continued involvement of clients in case-planning activities (Stein et al., 1978). Social workers differ in terms of how they choose to spend their time. For example, in the Alameda Project (see description in later section) agency staff spent much more time with foster parents than did project staff (Stein et al., 1978). The choices workers make as to how to distribute their time will influence outcomes they attain.

The professional literature, social science knowledge, statutory law, and agency policy provide guidance for selection of decision-making criteria and rules.

SOCIAL WORK LITERATURE

The value of the professional literature as a guide for decision making has been mixed. Social workers are encouraged to gather information in a number of areas descriptive of a client's life. However, little guidance is offered as to how to use this information for making decisions. Efforts to provide guidelines can be found in projects that explore the comparative effectiveness of different decision-making frameworks. For example, studies in child welfare indicate that decision-making frameworks are available to increase continuity of care for children.

The Alameda Project was a two-year experiment designed to offer intensive services to the natural parents of children in foster care in order to arrive at planned decisions concerning the children's futures (Stein et al., 1978). Many more children in the experimental units were out of foster placements or were headed out at the end of two years, compared with children in the control unit. Continuity in living arrangements was achieved through restoration to natural parents, termination of parental rights with subsequent adoption, arranging for a court-appointed guardian or planned long-term care with written or verbal agreements between agency and foster parents. Written service agreements with clients were an important component of the case management procedures used in this project. In addition to their valve in predicting outcome, service agreements provide a framework within which case plans are carried out (see Chapter 3). Contracts guide decision-making tasks by reminding participants of points when alternatives should be considered. The reaction of clients who signed service agreements during the Alameda Project were overwhelmingly positive. Clients often remarked that the content of the written agreements was the first specific information they had received about what had to be done to work toward having a child returned to their care. Having a copy of the agreement at home provided a ready reference point to check what was expected on a daily or weekly basis. The clarity of these agreements was very positively received by juvenile court judges. The value of service agreements for case planning and prediction derives in large measure from the clarity with which they are written. If this value is to be realized, clear guidelines for writing such agreements must be used (see Chapter 3).

The Oregon Project demonstrated the effectiveness of a systematic case management procedure in securing termination of parental rights with subsequent adoption or guardianship for children who were in out-of-home care (Emlen et al., 1976, 1977). Fifteen workers provided services over a two-year period. Each carried an average caseload of 45 cases. Of 509 children initially identified as not likely to return home as of November 1, 1973, 26% (n - 131) had been returned to the care of their parents as of October 31, 1976; 36% (n - 184) had been adopted, and plans for adoption were in progress for 83 children; contractual foster care had been arranged for 37 children; and 15 had been placed with relatives.

That out-of-home placement may often be avoided is strikingly demonstrated by a study of children who were headed for institutional care in Massachusetts (Heck and Gruber, 1976). Rather than sending all these children to such care, they were randomly assigned to one of four groups. In two of the groups the children were returned home, and intensive services were provided to biological parents and their children. In one of these groups services were based on a behavioral framework (n - 55) and in the other it was based on a psychodynamic framework (n - 59). A third group of children received consultation services from the Treatment Alternatives Project at intake only and were then referred to residential care, and a fourth group of children (n - 45) were referred to residential care without any services by the project. A much smaller proportion of the children in groups 1 and 2 were placed in institutional settings, compared to children in groups 3 and 4, who remained in care of the Division of Family and Children Services. The costs involved for the intensive services provided to children in groups 1 and 2 were no more than the state would normally have spent on residential care. In fact, the project "treated one-third greater a caseload than did the Department for the amount of money designated" (Heck and Gruber, 1976: 245). The advantages of using a systematic decision-making procedure has been explored in relation to other populations as well (Clark et al., 1980).

The Oregon and Alameda Projects developed guidelines for decision making for children for whom out-of-home placement decisions had already been made. Neither project dealt with the intake process and the critical decisions made during that process. The goal of the Illinois/ West Virginia project was to develop a framework for decision making at intake. Guidelines for making intake decisions would, when combined with the methods developed and tested during the Alameda and Oregon Projects, provide guidance for child welfare staff in making all decisions from the point of initial contact through case termination (Stein and Rzepnicki, forthcoming).

The decision-making procedures developed in the Illinois/West Virginia project were field tested for one year in two public welfare agencies in two states and in one voluntary agency. Cases were randomly assigned to experimental and control units by intake supervisors. Control workers used their traditional approach to decision making. Results showed the utility of a structured decision-making framework. Experimental workers spent significantly less time than did control staff in decision-making activities, which included gathering information, consultation with supervisors and colleagues, analyzing data to reach decisions and private thinking time about decisions.

Cases were tracked from intake into service units. Service workers reported data on time spent in decision-making activities. These workers spent significantly less time in decision-making activities when their cases came from experimental workers than when they came from control staff. Service workers evaluated the information provided by experimental intake staff as more useful for decision making than the information provided by control workers. Staff reported that the structured decision-making procedures were very useful and that they were satisfied with them. Use of a structured approach to decision making increased their sense of competence since the framework described the minimum information required to make each decision and provided guidance for using information. Workers reported that they were better able to justify their decisions to supervisors, juvenile court officers, and colleagues than had been the case in the past. There were no differences between experimental and control unit cases in recidivism.

SOCIAL SCIENCE LITERATURE

We know more today than we did even ten years ago about how people influence and are influenced by their environment. We have learned that our ability to make long-range predictions about human behavior is limited. Recently a great deal of attention has been devoted to exploration of the ways in which social networks and social support systems influence health and behavior (e.g., Gottlieb, 1981) and sources of error that influence the social judgments we make (e.g., Nisbett and Ross, 1980). Greater attention has been devoted to identification of characteristics common to diverse helping frameworks (e.g., Goldfried, 1980).

Organizational variables influence service delivery. It is impossible to understand the decisions made by line staff and supervisors without considering the role of factors such as clarity of agency objectives and how incentives are distributed. Use of effective procedures by line staff requires facilitative supervisory and administrative arrangements. Just as there is more information available now, compared to a few years ago, concerning how to help clients, more information is also available concerning effective supervisory and administrative practices. We know more about the importance of consistent incentives in maintaining effective practice. (See Chapter 7.)

Information from these sources as well as other related areas in the social sciences should be used in designing decision-making procedures in social work.

STATUTORY LAW AND AGENCY POLICY

Legal and policy requirements must be considered in the development of a framework for decision making. These may call for certain kinds of information as a basis for selecting options and may limit autonomy in decision making. Before a client can be placed in a restrictive setting, for instance, a worker may need psychiatric testimony to the effect that the client would pose a danger to others if left in the community. Without such evidence, placement in a restrictive setting may not be possible, despite the worker's judgments that it is appropriate. The law limits conditions under which intervention may occur with nonvoluntary clients. Court decisions may define the population of clients who must participate in decision making. For example, courts have recognized the right of foster parents to participate in decisions made for children who have been in their custody for long periods of time. A procedural manual for judicial review provides judges with a set of questions to ask biological parents to ensure that they have participated in case planning and that they understand the case plan and agree with its contents. Court rulings regarding evidence must be considered in developing procedures for decision making. For example, in 1982 the United States Supreme Court changed the standard for evidence for termination of parental rights from the less stringent "preponderance of evidence," to a requirement for "clear and convincing evidence."

Agency policy should offer direction to you and your staff in making critical choices. Policy should identify the population of clients to be served and eligibility criteria for service. Agency policy may restrict case-planning options. In child welfare, for example, the policies of many agencies reflecting new federal law, require that initial case plans describe procedures for maintaining children in their own homes. Except in cases in which emergency removal is necessary, maintaining children in their own homes must be the first planning option. If removal is necessary, family reunification must be the planning goal. You may have to take an active role in requesting more explicit policy guidelines concerning criteria and rules to consider in making decisions and ensuring that decisions made by staff take account of court decisions and statutory law. You will have to offer consultation to staff to assist them in making difficult decisions and routinely review case records to ensure that agency goals are pursued.

PRACTICE TASK 1.4

Write two examples of decisions that your workers have to make. Then, write down factors that *should* influence these decisions. Finally, check the items you mention that are supported by research.

OUR VALUES

We consider the main concern in social work to be the client. Thus, in assessing the use of any assessment or intervention procedure, or supervisory or administrative process, our first criterion is what is best for offering effective services to clients. Although all social workers may agree with this statement at such a general level, when specific examples are discussed, agreement may not be complete. For example, a worker may object to having the quality of her work assessed; she may insist that this infringes on her rights as a professional. Here we would consider accountability to clients uppermost and would consider the obligation to monitor quality of service compelling — doing so, of course, in a way that is helpful and positive and protective of the legitimate concerns of the worker.

Another situation in which agreement might not be found is one in which worker preference for a procedure is not supported by empirical data. Let's say that method A has been shown to be more effective than method B with clients with a given concern, but the worker prefers B because she feels it is more effective. The criterion of accountability to clients constrains workers to use the "best validated method" (Davison and Stuart, 1975), that is, the method that has the strongest empirical support in relation to effects achieved. Accountability to clients does place limits on worker discretion. Some constraints, such as using the least intrusive intervention, are now legally mandated.

Most supervisors would agree that they share responsibility for ensuring that effective services are offered to clients. Kadushin (1976: 55) states that careful monitoring is "an inescapable function" of supervisors. Some supervisors may not believe that they are responsible for evaluating the quality of services offered by their staff. They may align themselves with unit workers and consider evaluation the task of higher administration. Or they may believe that they have no right to evaluate, that staff can and will adequately monitor the quality of their work, or that casework is an art, essentially undefinable, so that we cannot know what to examine in terms of process or outcome. Some staff do monitor the quality of their work, and the framework presented in this manual is designed to gradually give line staff more responsibility for evaluation. However, additional checks are necessary to ensure high quality service. Skill deficits of staff will have to be identified and learning opportunities provided through inservice training, consultation, or supervisory guidance. Many components of effective practice are identifiable, and it is possible to establish criteria for judging whether these have been offered.

All too often, process has been artificially separated from outcome in that only one or the other is examined. For example, many studies examining the effectiveness of casework services look only at outcome and ignore process (the procedures employed). Only if both process and outcome are examined can we increase our knowledge about the relationship of given procedures to outcome. Guidelines that can be used to review both process and outcome are described in this book. Examination of the quality of services offered by your staff will help you to ensure that effective services are offered to clients. This will also offer information about training needs of your staff.

Decisions can be made actively or passively. That is, a decision can be made by not making a decision — just letting time pass. You may believe that you cannot gain an overview of all cases on your unit in order to plan priorities more effectively, or you may believe that if time passes, priorities will work themselves out. Not making a decision is a decision. That systematic decision-making procedures are necessary is suggested by findings that clients often enter out-of-home care unnecessarily and often drift in long-term care, by the frequent suggestion that a decision-making framework is needed, and by studies reporting the high number of clients without case plans. We urge you to make active rather than passive decisions.

PRACTICE TASK **1.5**

Identify two passive decisions that you have made over the past month. Would the quality of service offered be better if you had made active decisions?

Chapter 2

INTAKE AND INITIAL CASE PLANNING

Decisions must be made about whom to accept as clients and whom to reject or refer elsewhere. These decisions will be influenced by the service delivery goals of your agency which, in turn, are influenced by funding sources and legislation. Decisions must be made as to whether applicants can satisfy eligibility requirements for certain services and whether your agency is the most suitable source for a client. Criteria used in making such decisions should be clearly defined and equitably used across clients. However, criteria are often *not* clearly defined nor employed equitably. Personal preferences and attitudes of individual social workers often influence intake decisions. A focus on the pathology of applicants rather than upon their assets increases the likelihood that social workers will recommend acceptance of a case and intervention. Decisions made at intake are of critical importance. The choices made can set the course for future transactions between workers and clients in your agency as well as those between clients and service providers in other agencies. Once accepted by an agency, a series of other events may occur, which may or may not benefit applicants. Children or adults may be placed in out-of-home care even though this is not necessary. Once there, they may remain in care for an unnecessarily long time. Failure of the administration to clearly define the limits of service delivery will result in individuals' acceptance for services that should be provided by other agencies, thus straining the resources of an agency to satisfy its service mandates. Decisions made by social workers — e.g., whether to conduct an assessment in the office, in the client's home, or both, whether to gather information through verbal exchanges during interviews, through observation of family members at home, or through a combination of methods — will influence the quality of information collected (see Chapter 4). Information gathered during initial assessment provides the basis for a decision about whether to open a case and will also influence the nature of services provided.

An overview of the intake process is presented below, followed by a detailed discussion of each phase of intake. Issues of concern to supervisors are highlighted. A framework for review of intake decisions made by staff is presented.

PRACTICE TASK 2.1

Identify criteria used in your agency to make intake decisions. Are these clear? Do you think these are the best criteria to use? If not, what changes should be made?

AN OVERVIEW OF INTAKE

Intake is defined here as a process beginning with initial contact with a client, applicant, or resistor (Perlman, 1979) and ending with the development of a case plan. The goal of intake is to determine whether a case is appropriate for agency services. If it is, an initial case plan is designed. Intake begins with an *initial screening*, during which workers find out why the client has come or been referred to the agency. Outcomes of initial screening include referring clients to other agencies, and accepting cases for service while continuing others in the intake process. When clients are continued at intake, a *preliminary assessment* takes place. The goal of this assessment is to gather data that permits description of concerns in precise terms, allowing for a determination of what services are needed and whether to provide them in the host agency or to refer the client elsewhere. A series of decisions must be made in the course of assessment. These include where to gather information, the best method of acquiring information, the role of the worker, the client and significant others during the assessment process, and whether assistance is needed from professionals with specialized skills (such as medical or legal personnel).

Intake concludes with the design of an *initial case plan*. Decisions must be made as to the long-range goal of a plan, objectives that must be achieved to reach this goal, the interventions that will be used to achieve objectives, and who will provide services. If collaterals are involved in service provision, a framework for coordinating services must be negotiated (see Chapter 6). Intake workers may make a series of additional decisions, depending upon the area of service. Staff who provide child protective services, for instance, have to decide whether a child is in immediate danger and, if so, whether the child can be safeguarded at home or should be taken into protective custody and whether it is necessary to petition the court. Building a a *case record* is a central activity that occurs during all stages of the intake process.

INITIAL SCREENING

Initial screening should be completed by the end of one, or at most two, interviews. This may result in (1) referring clients to other agencies; (2) referring clients to an agency worker who is currently managing the client's case or involving the case manager in the decision-making process; (3) accepting a case for service; or (4) gathering additional information in order to make a decision. The latter course of action may require involving others whose expertise is needed to determine eligibility. Clients may be referred elsewhere because the agency does not offer services requested, because there are no openings in the service area requested, or because clients do not meet eligibility requirements.

Some clients will request a specific service, for example, day-care or family planning. Others will refer to problems with vague statements such as, "I am depressed," or "My partner and I can't get along." Social workers must match expressed concerns with given services and decide whether to continue the case at intake or refer the client elsewhere. You should caution your staff against hasty matching of problems and services. A client's request may be inappropriate for your agency. Since clients often express problems in general terms, assessment information beyond what is gathered in the initial interview may be needed before a determination can be made whether to provide services or to refer the client elsewhere.

After determining the type of assistance required, intake staff should find out whether the client is currently receiving services from their agency. If a case is active in the agency, the worker who is managing the case should participate in the decision to continue intake or to refer the client. There are several reasons for involving workers who are managing a case at this point. The likelihood of duplication of services is reduced, since the current worker will have an overview of services the client is receiving. Second, the client's case manager is responsible for coordinating the activities of all service providers. A framework for coordination should be negotiated at the time a referral is made. The current worker may have assessment information that can help to clarify desired outcomes. Using available data saves both worker and client time. Finally, information available to the case manager may suggest the superiority of one intervention approach. This increases the likelihood of making an appropriate referral if more than one option is available.

If cases are continued at intake, workers must consider whether they need assistance to determine client eligibility. Access to some services may be contingent upon whether the client is receiving other services. For example, whether a mother is receiving Aid to Families with Dependent Children (AFDC) or is eligible for AFDC may influence eligibility for day-care or homemaker service. An intake worker may request assistance from an eligibility worker. Workers should have access to a directory of current services offered by their agency and a list of services offered by other community agencies. Eligibility requirements for each service should be listed and information regarding space available for each service should be noted and updated on a regular basis.

You should monitor the decisions make at the end of the initial screening period. There are costs to both clients and to the agency if inappropriate referrals are made or if cases are continued at intake when they should be referred elsewhere. Clients at risk may not receive needed services if incorrect referrals are made. They may be turned away by the agency and "slip through the cracks" of the service delivery system. Continuing clients for ongoing intake when they should be referred to other agencies is wasteful of resources and intrusive for clients who will be subjected to unnecessary duplication of assessment efforts.

You can gain an overview of decisions made by intake workers from review of the form shown in Figure 2.1. For each client interviewed, workers enter the client's name, the service requested or problem(s) identified, and they place a check mark in the appropriate column describing the outcome of initial screening. Data can be collected at the end of each week to show the number and percentage of clients by each outcome category.

This information has several uses. Collected over time, this offers a baseline against which future reports can be evaluated. Second, variations in a unit may suggest a developing trend, for example, an increase in certain types of requests because of high unemployment. Third, this will indicate whether there are marked variations among workers in services requested, problems identified, and case dispositions. If decisions made by a certain worker differ considerably from those of other workers, this will provide a cue to conduct a

CASE NAME	SERVICE REQUIRED	PROBLEMS IDENTIFIED	OUTCOME					
			INFORMATION ONLY	REFERRED			CONTINUED FOR ASSESSMENT	ACCEPTED AT INITIAL SCREENING
				SERVICE NOT OFFERED	CLIENT NOT ELIGIBLE	SPACE NOT AVAILABLE		

Figure 2.1 Initial Screening

detailed review of the worker's records. Questions of concern include the following:

(1)   Are client requests interpreted correctly? For example, if the client states a problem in vague terms, "I am unhappy," does the worker fail to clarify this general complaint before assigning this problem to a service category?

(2)   If the client was referred, does the referral made indicate effective use of a service directory? That is, was the client referred to an agency offering the correct service?

(3)   Has the worker requested needed assistance to determine eligibility? For instance, if the service requires a determination of income eligibility, does the record show that an eligibility worker was consulted?

(4)   If the case is active in the agency, does the record show that the worker carrying the case or the worker's supervisor was involved in the decision to accept the case or to refer?

PRACTICE TASK 2.2

Describe how intake decisions are evaluated in your agency. Is this procedure adequate? If not, how could it be improved?

PRACTICE TASK 2.3

Identify errors made by workers concerning intake decisions. How could these be avoided?

BUILDING A CASE RECORD

The case record is begun at intake. The information compiled by intake staff sets the stage for future transactions between clients and social service personnel, who often rely on the data recorded to make subsequent decisions. You should ensure that documentation is complete — for example, that information necessary to reach a decision has been recorded and that workers record in a *descriptive* manner, that is, report observations, as well as inferences. Direct quotations and descriptive accounts phrased in the first person should be used. Examples include statements such as "Mr. King said that he is afraid of losing his home when his unemployment benefits run out," and, "I observed Larry Hayens, aged 5, playing unattended in an unenclosed area six feet from the roadway."

If there are gaps in information or if material is recorded in an inferential, rather than descriptive, manner requiring others to subjectively interpret material, continuity in service provision is unlikely. Some or all of the assessment process may have to be repeated to acquire needed information, or inappropriate services may be offered. Client involvement in decision making is partly contingent upon the client's ability to understand written material. Workers should clearly describe their observations and should clearly describe the rationale for choices they make.

PRACTICE TASK 2.4

Select a few case records written by your workers and examine these using the following criteria: (1) Are inferences supported by descriptive data? (2) Are rationales for decisions clearly described? (3) Is the documentation for decisions made complete?

Guidelines should be provided to workers to help them to determine what data to gather at each stage of the intake process. There are three levels of information that are used for deciding whether agency services will be offered. First, there is general information consisting of labels used to describe problems such as "I am depressed," "My child is unmanageable," "He beats his daughter," and so forth. Examples of the behaviors, thoughts, and feelings referred to by these general labels and information regarding related circumstances make up a second level of information. This information gives direction to the process of conducting an in-depth assessment during which detailed data required to identify appropriate intervention strategies are gathered (level 3). Use of standardized recording forms increases the likelihood that staff will record information needed for effective decision making. Standardized forms include problem profiles, a record of current and prior use of services, case logs, and narrative outlines.

PRACTICE TASK 2.5

Describe guidelines you offer to your staff for case recording.

PROBLEM PROFILES

Problem profiles can be used to record an overview of difficulties reported by clients and referring sources. (Gambrill et al., 1971). Examples of the behaviors, thoughts, or feelings that define concerns are recorded as well as related factors (what happens right before and after problematic reactions), such as reactions of significant others (see example in Chapter 3).

Recording examples and situations indicates contexts in which it would be useful to gather additional assessment data and indicates significant others who should be interviewed. Client and family strengths in relation to each concern are also noted. Information regarding assets adds perspective to what otherwise might be an overly pessimistic view of situations. Information describing assets is important in arriving at a decision whether to provide services or to refer clients elsewhere.

PRACTICE TASK **2.6**

Make up copies of a problem profile form and explain the value of this form to your workers (see Figure 3.1). Ask them if they would be willing to try out this form with one of their new cases.

CURRENT AND PRIOR USE OF SERVICES

Current and prior use of services should be noted. Part I of Figure 2.2 includes a checklist of services such as AFDC, day-care, counseling for marital problems, and foster home services. For each service received, workers check whether use is current or past (if past, the date the case was closed is also noted), the name of the worker or supervisor who managed the case, and the name of the service recipient if different from the family name. The second part of the form is completed if clients are receiving or have received services from other community agencies. If they have, the agency is identified and its address and phone number are recorded. The service dates are listed, as is the name of the person who provided the service, the problems addressed, and the services offered to address concerns. Information on this form is used to locate sources of helpful information. This form is not meant to be used to record detailed information describing problems and interventions. Detailed material will be gathered later, with the client's permission, if services are offered and the information seems relevant to current problems.

PART I   (1) Is the client/family currently receiving services from the agency? Yes _____ No _____
(2) If no, has the client/family received services within the last two years? Yes _____ No _____
(3) If yes to 1 or 2, complete the following then go to Part II. If no to 1 and 2, go directly to Part II.

Service	Use		If past, date closed	Name of		Name of Service Recipient If Different Than Family Name
	Current	Past		Worker	Supervisor	
1. financial (insert type in #2, e.g. AFDC, G.A.)						
2. _____						
3. food stamps						
4. medicare						
5. medicaid						
6. day-care						
7. homemaker						
8. protective service						
9. foster care						
10. adoption						
11. other (insert type)						

PART II   (1) Is the client/family receiving services from another community agency? Yes _____ No _____
(2) If no, has the client/family received services within the last 2 years? Yes _____ No _____
(3) If yes 1 or 2, complete the following and request permission to contact the resource to learn about the services provided.
(4) If no to 1 and 2, do not complete this form.

Agencies	Service Dates		Name of Counselor/ Worker	Problems Addressed	Services Provided
	From	To			
1. Name _____ Address _____ Telephone _____					
2. Name _____ Address _____ Telephone _____					
3. Name _____ Address _____ Telephone _____					

SOURCE: T. J. Stein and T. L. Rzepnicki, *Decision Making at Child Welfare Intake: A Handbook for Practitioners* (pp. 68-69). Copyright © 1983 by the Child Welfare League of America. Reprinted by permission.

Figure 2.2   Information Regarding Use of Services

Information in agency records as well as that provided by other service providers can be useful in decision making. Collateral resources may have information that is related to a service request. A public health nurse might have detailed information about a parent's child-care skills, including information regarding skill deficits. It would be wasteful of resources for a worker to undertake or arrange for an assessment that would duplicate information already available. Knowledge of services currently being provided and information regarding the efficacy of prior services will be helpful in selecting intervention strategies. Approaches that were not effective can be eliminated and effective approaches may be tried again.

The value of case records depends upon their age and data noted. Vague records may be of little value. When information is old, even if it is descriptive, it may be of limited use.

PRACTICE TASK 2.7

Make up copies of the form describing Information Regarding Use of Services. Explain the rationale for using this form and ask your workers to complete this form for two of their cases.

CASE LOGS

A case log, in which all contacts made with and on behalf of a client are recorded, should be begun at intake. This should include the date, type of contact (e.g., in office, home), who was present, duration of contact, and main goal and outcome. This information provides a running account of all transactions between staff, clients, collaterals, and significant others, such as relatives, friends, and neighbors of the family.

PRACTICE TASK 2.8

Make up copies of case logs and ask your staff to keep these in two of their cases.

NARRATIVE RECORDING

Process or narrative recording is commonly used by social workers. The purpose of such recording is to provide detailed information regarding problems and related factors. This type of recording often takes the form of free flowing narratives, which are of little value. Inferences are often recorded with no descriptive information on which such inferences are based. The use of labels such as quarrelsome, depressed, and unmanageable — without inclusion of the behavior to which such labels refer — offers little information of value. Redundancies and missing information further reduce the value of narrative records. Inclusion of topical headings on a narrative form can encourage staff to record helpful information. Training will have to be provided to staff as needed to enhance skills in recording clear descriptions of problems and related factors, as well as assets. Detailed information regarding each problem listed on the problem profile can be recorded under these topical headings. This narrative recording form can be used during assessment interviews to record information provided by such significant others as family members. It should be used in conjunction with observational recording forms (see Chapter 4) and with problem profiles. If new problems are identified or additional behavioral examples, situational factors, or client strengths reported for problems already on the profile, this information can be added to the profile. Narrative recording allows for recording of information that is too detailed to be included on a problem profile. Topics and information recorded under each are described below.

Views of significant others about problems listed on the profile. The problem profile should be shared with significant others and their input gained about whether they view items noted on the profile as troublesome, whether they agree with the behavioral and situational examples offered, and whether they have concerns they would like to add to the profile (if so, these should be added). Their view of strengths related to concerns should also be noted. Information provided by significant others can add perspectives on problems that may be missing when input is gained from only one person. For example, disagreements about problems among family members is important information.

Information regarding the history of the problem and services used in relation to the problem. Workers should determine whether a problem is a long-standing one or whether this is of recent origin. Was a problem triggered by an identifiable event? For example, did the birth of a child, loss of employment, separation from a mate, or death of a partner precipitate a crisis? Or, did a recent crisis force clients to cope with a long standing problem? Knowing whether a problem was precipitated by a crisis or is the result of a characteristic set of interaction patterns is important in selecting appropriate interventions. Knowledge of services offered in the past for similar problems and information regarding the effects of services provided is also important (see Figure 2.2).

Client interaction with significant others. Patterns of interaction that hint at problematic dynamics may be observed. For instance, a parent who has requested services may describe her son as unmanageable. Examples offered might include interrupting her and refusing to follow her instructions. The worker may observe that the parent interrupts her son each time he tries to say something; the parent is modeling the behavior she finds distasteful. The worker may hypothesize that interruptions on the part of her son are encouraged by such parental examples. This hypothesis, and the observations upon which it is based, should be noted in the narrative record.

Additional assets. Positive feelings family members display toward each other, respect shown through attentive listening behavior, and demonstrated parenting skills (among other observations) should be recorded. Information regarding significant others — relatives or friends, for example — whose aid might be solicited during assessment or intervention should be gathered.

Changes clients would like to make as a result of participation in service delivery programs. These should be identified, perhaps on the problem profile (see Chapter 3). Workers must attend to whether expectations are realistic. Does a client expect that, as an outcome of a service program, he will feel good all of the time? Does a parent expect that a 16-year-old will obey all instructions without argument? Client expectations offer guidelines concerning possible intervention strategies. For example, a client who reports that she is depressed may, when asked what she expects from services (or what she would be doing if she were not depressed) may report that she would like to spend more time with other people. Increasing interaction with others may become the objective of service provision.

You should monitor the quality of records kept by staff. Questions to bear in mind when reviewing records include the following: (1) Has the worker completed all necessary forms? (2) Has the worker provided relevant information in all categories? (3) Is the writing descriptive? A good test for this is to have two people independently read the material and report what they would have seen had they been present. The degree of agreement obtained will reflect the clarity of the recorded information.

Staff should understand the ways in which information recorded on different forms contributes to clarification of problems, to decisions whether to offer services, and what services to offer. Problems listed on the problem profile set the stage for subsequent work. The profile contains a summary and overview of the reasons services were requested and offers guidelines for further assessment efforts — for example, what contexts to explore; what to watch for in these settings, and who else to talk to. Services received currently or in the past related to each problem listed should be recorded on another form. This information serves as a reminder of potential sources of additional information regarding services offered and outcomes achieved. The description of transactions with and on behalf of clients recorded on case logs is very helpful in reviewing workers' efforts to assist clients. If clients consistently fail to maintain appointments, the log may be the only source of documentation of efforts to provide assistance. Case narratives contain detailed information regarding problems summarized on the problem profile. The information recorded in the narrative, problem profile, and information from other service providers should be helpful in selecting methods for continued assessment (such as direct observation of clients in their natural environment) and in deciding whether assistance is needed from others in gathering assessment data.

PRACTICE TASK 2.9

Review the intake forms used by your workers. Describe how these could be improved.

DECIDING WHETHER ASSISTANCE IS NEEDED WITH ASSESSMENT

Assessment may be beyond the skills of one person. The expertise of medical personnel, attorneys, psychologists, and psychiatrists, in addition to those of the social worker may be required to determine the exact nature of difficulties and related factors and to select promising interventions. Workers may lack experience in gathering helpful information based on direct observation of interaction between clients, such as between a parent and child or husband and wife. Workers may lack skills in developing self-monitoring forms for client use (see Chapter 4). You may have to provide help with such tasks. Decisions to request help with assessment may be made at any time during the assessment process. For example, based on observations during a home visit, a worker may ask for assistance from a public health nurse to assess a parent's child-care knowledge and skills.

PRACTICE TASK **2.10**

Identify what kinds of assistance your workers often need with assssment. Who provides this? Could the assistance be improved any way?

MAKING REFERRALS AND FOLLOW-UP

Agencies differ in their policies regarding how referrals are made and whether referrals are followed up. At one extreme, clients are simply given the name, address, and telephone number of an agency and are expected to follow through with contacting the agency on their own. Alternatively, appointments may be made for clients with staff in another agency and follow-ups made to determine if agency services have been sought and what happened.

If assessment of concerns and related factors is completed prior to a referral, then referrals can be made in a more informed manner since more information is available. This will increase the likelihood of making appropriate referrals. For example, data gathered during assessment may indicate that child-management problems are related to marital problems. An agency offering effective services in both areas could then be selected, if one is available. You should monitor referrals to ensure that proper procedures are followed. You could make this task feasible by selecting a sample of cases to review.

PRACTICE TASK **2.11**

Describe how you monitor the quality of referrals made by your workers as well as how you could improve this procedure with minimal time and effort.

DECIDING WHETHER TO OPEN A CASE
FOR AGENCY SERVICES

The decision about whether to open a case for agency services or to refer a case elsewhere depends on several factors. An agency's service mandate is foremost. Intake staff are often handicapped in making decisions by vague or overly broad policy statements. Overly broad service mandates may do more harm than good. The conditions necessary for realizing the ideal of serving all comers — a sufficient number of staff to handle requests and the availability of any service in sufficient quantity to meet consumer demand — are rarely present. The costs involved when caseloads are so high that even the most skilled practitioners do not have sufficient time to provide effective service, or to coordinate those offered by others, must be considered. Persons with the greatest need may not receive necessary services.

Because of your intermediate position between line workers and higher levels of administration, you may be in the best position to advocate specific policy guidelines for intake. You could, for example, document the number of underserved and unserved cases and note the real or hypothetical consequences for clients. For instance, children may have been placed in foster care or be at risk of placement if day-care or homemaker services are not available. Information should be compiled on services frequently requested and deficits in space available. Records should be monitored to ensure that staff document services requested and services offered, and services needed but unavailable. Information regarding deficits in services is invaluable in resource planning.

Agency policy should provide guidance for setting priorities concerning cases to be served. Preference should be given to clients at greatest risk. For example, if assessment shows that a depressed client has ceased to carry out child-care tasks to the point of neglecting a child who lacks self-help skills or who is too young to engage in self-help behavior, it is reasonable to hypothesize that the child is at risk and to support an argument for providing service. Likewise, assessment may show that two adults spend the majority of their time together quarreling. Data collected may indicate that they have made efforts to resolve their difficulties without professional help, for example, through participation in a self-help couples group and that they are now asking for professional assistance as a last resort. The suggestion that they are at risk of separation or divorce may be plausible based on such information.

The formation of "risk hypotheses" has been shown to be useful in deciding what cases to serve in voluntary child welfare programs (Stein and Rzepnicki, in press). The utility of such hypotheses requires that present dangers be focused on. Long-range predictions that cannot be supported by currently available knowledge should be discouraged. To suggest, for instance, that a child whose behavior at home and at school is within acceptable boundaries is at risk of emotional disturbance because his parents are divorcing, goes beyond what the facts would support (see for example Skolnick, 1978; White et al., 1973; Goldstein, Freud, and Solnit, 1973).

PRACTICE TASK 2.12

Identify types of risk that are important to consider in your agency's work with clients. What methods do your workers use to balance risks in each case?

Eligibility criteria, such as income considerations, may enter into the decision-making process. Whether staff have the skills to provide services to clients who meet policy and eligibility criteria should also be considered. You should be aware of the problem-solving skills of your staff, and consider the likelihood of their providing the most effective service or whether clients could receive more effective services from another agency.

PRACTICE TASK 2.13

What information do you use to determine whether staff have required skills to offer services?

Correct problem specification is essential in deciding whether to accept cases for agency service or to refer clients to other community resources. The categories used to explain why cases are opened, such as "depression" or "marital conflict," do not provide sufficient information for identifying intervention strategies since such concerns may be related to many different factors. Depression, for instance, may result from a lack of social contacts which, in turn, may result from lack of knowledge about where to meet people, lack of skills for engaging others in conversation, or negative self-statements such as, "No one would be interested in meeting me." Having sole responsibility for child care and household management or loss of employment may also be related to depression. Statements about being depressed may be encouraged by attention from significant others. Different maintaining conditions may require different intervention strategies.

You should arrange training for staff who lack knowledge or skills in problem definition, provide assistance as needed regarding appropriate assessment methods, and monitor assessment procedures used by staff.

SETTING PRIORITIES

You should make sure that your workers have guidelines for setting priorities among problems and that these are followed. Resolution of some problems — for example, those requiring financial, medical, or housing assistance — may involve only a few client tasks, such as completion of forms for eligibility determination, in contrast to problems that require attendance at counseling sessions over a period of weeks. Simultaneous intervention on many problems that require many client tasks can be overwhelming. Some guidelines for setting priorities are described below.

(1) Priority should be given to problems that create risk for clients, where risk is defined to include violence between family members, separation or divorce, or removal of children from own homes. Determination of risk may be made based on information recorded on a problem profile and from other initial assessment information such as that recorded in case narratives and information provided by collateral resources. Examples include need for medical, housing or financial assistance. There may be past evidence of child abuse, supporting a hypothesis of further injury without immediate services. In other instances, continued assessment will be required before a determination can be made.

(2) Some problems must be addressed before others can be resolved. If a client has an alcohol problem that is incapacitating, as well as deficits in work skills, the former will require attention before the latter can be dealt with

(3) The court may require certain problems to be addressed. A judge, for instance, may require parents to attend counseling sessions. Workers should request the court to rescind or modify treatment orders if there is evidence to suggest that a service is not likely to produce the desired outcome or that there is another service more likely to facilitate goal attainment. If a judge is unwilling to rescind or modify a treatment order, however, the judicial stipulation will have to be addressed.

(4) A lack of resources can influence priorities. For example, there may be no space available in a desired program and no other alternatives.

PRACTICE TASK **2.14**

Review written statements by your agency describing agency priorities. Are these clear? Write a brief memo to your staff describing priorities in clear terms.

INITIAL CASE PLANNING

When clients are accepted for agency service the intake worker, the client, and the worker to whom the case will be transferred should develop an initial case plan. Case plans describe long-range goals, problem-solving objectives, the procedure to be followed to achieve objectives, and the time frame for attaining objectives. Individuals responsible for service provision are identified and a framework for collaboration established. Collaboration between the intake worker, who is familiar with the case (and who may have established a working relationship with the client), and the worker who will bear responsibility for service provision will facilitate a smooth transition for the client.

If assessment is not complete, information required to identify objectives may not be available at the end of intake. For example, it may be clear that a case is appropriate for agency services, but antecedent and maintaining conditions may not have been specified precisely enough to identify objectives. When this occurs the goal of the service agreement is to identify problems that should be addressed and to describe the procedures that will be used to complete assessment. Thus, initial service agreements may set forth the conditions for ongoing assessment and also describe certain problem-solving objectives. In some service settings, long-range goals may be determined by agency policy. For example, in child welfare agencies, policy may dictate that maintaining children in their own homes must be the goal of an initial case plan or, if children are removed under emergency conditions, restoration to their family of origin may be required as a first case goal. Decision-making steps involved in offering services within different outcome categories are described in the next chapter.

SUMMARY

Decisions made at intake set the course for future transactions. Initial screening may result in acceptance of applicants for services, referral of applicants to other sources, or gathering of additional information in order to make a decision. You should monitor the decisions made at the end of the initial screening period. This can be done by reviewing case records. Important components of records include an overview of problem areas, information concerning current and prior use of services, a case log noting all contacts with and on behalf of clients, and narrative records. Workers should have clear guidelines for setting priorities for service delivery as well as for information to include in case records.

Chapter 3

EVALUATING THE
QUALITY OF DECISION MAKING
WITHIN OUTCOME CATEGORIES

Categorizing cases in terms of outcome pursued is important if some outcomes are more critical than others. This offers information about how many cases are present in which no plans have been made, even after there has been ample time to do so. Another rationale for categorizing cases by outcome is that different decision-making steps are often involved in offering services within different outcome categories. For example, the steps a worker should move through in working with families to prevent out-of-home care of children differs from those involved in cases in which children have already been removed from their homes and placed in foster care. Seeking *changes* in behaviors or situations may require a different sequence of decisions than *maintaining* a person at a given level of functioning (Miller and Pruger, 1979). The steps involved in systematic decision making can serve as a framework for reviewing the quality of services provided. Each step toward goal attainment may be viewed as a checkpoint for monitoring progress. The outcome categories that are relevant will differ in different types of social service agencies. Examples are offered in this chapter that describe decision-making frameworks related to outcomes involved in offering services to children and their families in protective service units. Generic principles and steps are highlighted.

EXAMPLES OF OUTCOME CATEGORIES

Prevention of unnecessary out-of-home placement is an important goal in social work. Achieving this goal may require pursuit of both change and maintenance goals. For example, in order to maintain an elderly person in their home, effective intervention strategies may have to be designed (1) to maintain current levels of independent physical functioning (e.g., ensuring nutritional meals), and (2) to change goals (e.g., helping an elderly person and her children to develop more constructive problem-solving skills). Protective service workers for children are mandated to offer services in the home whenever this would not result in undue risk to a child. Practical reasons related to this mandate include the fact that it is easier to gather accurate assessment data in real-life settings. Second, problems of generalizing gains made are not as problematic when intervention is carried out in the clients' natural environment, such as their homes. Another outcome category that is relevant in most social work settings is that of long-term care — situations in which pursuit of change or maintenance goals may require ongoing services over a long period of time. For example, many children in child welfare are headed for long-term care, meaning that they will remain under state care until maturity. Clients may not know what outcome they wish to pursue. In such cases the goal selected may be to form a plan. Other outcome categories of relevance within protective service settings for children include restoration of children to the home of their biological parents, termination of parental rights with subsequent adoption or guardianship, and emancipation (the child reaches the age of 18 and is on his own).

We would like to emphasize the importance of allowing *clients* to select the overall goal. Unless they select the goal, the workers will be in the unenviable position of working toward outcomes that are not of value to clients. This will sharply decrease the likelihood of client participation. On the other hand, if the client selects the overall goal, all efforts on the part of workers are aimed toward a goal that the client states is a desired one. The outcome selected must of course be ethically acceptable to the worker. We would also like to emphasize that selection of an outcome category, such as return of a child from foster care to the home of her biological parents, offers no guarantee that this outcome will be achieved. This will depend on the participation by clients, the skills of the worker and involved collaterals, resources available, and problems that must be resolved to achieve the overall goal. Workers sometimes try to decide whether a client's goal can be achieved without going through the required problem-solving steps. A worker may think that biological parents will never be able to resolve deficiencies related to removal of their children. However, only if they are given a chance to do so can the next steps — such as termination of parental rights and subsequent adoption — ethically be pursued.

PRACTICE TASK 3.1

List the major outcome categories that are important in your work.

GENERIC COMPONENTS OF PLANS MADE
TO ACHIEVE OUTCOMES

No matter what the outcome category, there are certain generic characteristics that plans should reflect. Plans should be guided by the goal selected by the client and worker. This represents the outcome category. The goal gives direction to subsequent efforts, such as gathering a problem profile, identification of personal and environmental resources, and identification of significant others who should be involved in the program. (The overall goal pursued could, of course, be renegotiated.) A written service agreement between client and worker should be formed. Components of such agreements include the goal agreed upon, the objectives required to achieve this goal, responsibilities of involved parties, consequences that will occur dependent upon whether or not objectives are attained, an agreed-upon time limit for accomplishing objectives, and the names of those who will sign the agreement (see example described later in this chapter).

The use of written service agreements has many advantages. These are helpful in clarifying mutual expectations. When tasks are written down it is more obvious whether or not these are clearly stated, and so participants can make an informed decision regarding agreement to the stated terms. Agreements should be signed by all parties to the agreement, and clients as well as the social worker should receive a copy of the agreement. If clients do not wish to sign the agreement, the reasons for their reluctance should be explored. This may reflect uncertainty about what outcome to pursue, and selection of outcome may required further discussion. Maybe a decision-making contract should be selected in which the goal is to help the client reach a decision. Some people may simply be reluctant to sign their name to any paper. Such individual differences should be respected. Some clients may not be able to read or see, in which instance material in the contract could be shared verbally.

The important point to remember about service agreements is that they are case-planning tools; they must be used flexibly and creatively. Two of their main functions are to ensure clarity of expectations between workers and clients and to discourage hidden agendas. By putting the goal and related objectives in writing and by describing the responsibilities of each party, each person is recognized as an integral part of the process of problem resolution. In addition, signing an agreement may increase a client's commitment to participate in efforts to make changes. Clients should receive a copy of the written agreement whether or not they sign this, since the steps required to accomplish the plans are usually the same.

Service agreements can be formed at different points. If they are formed at an early point — that is, before all objectives required to achieve a goal have been identified — they should describe the conditions necessary to complete assessment, such as observation of interaction between significant others. These agreements should also describe the responsibilities of the worker to help the client resolve any additional concerns that are identified. Intervention should be initiated in relation to clearly defined objectives while gathering additional assessment information concerning other areas. This will enable workers to offer immediate help with some problems while gathering needed information in other areas. Plans made to accomplish each objective should be attached to the service agreement as these are formed and copies given to the client. Plans should be based on an accurate description of problems and related objectives. For example, whenever possible, data should be gathered concerning the frequency of a problematic behavior (e.g., drinking) prior to intervention (e.g., when a person drinks, how much she drinks, and when she drinks). This information is useful in assessing progress during intervention, in identifying factors related to drinking, and deciding where to start an intervention program.

Intermediate steps that must be pursued to attain each objective should also be described. If one objective is to locate a new living space (e.g., to move from one room in a hotel to a two-bedroom apartment), intermediate steps required to accomplish this should be described — for instance, locating possible apartments and acquiring information about them. Identification of intermediate steps will allow workers to be sure that clients have the required skills to carry these out successfully and offers opportunities to support each step toward attaining an objective. (See Chapter 5 for further discussion.) Plans should include a clear description of how multiple services will be coordinated (see Chapter 6) and should describe a procedure for assessing progress, so that clients, significant others, and supervisors are able to determine readily the effects of intervention (see Chapter 5).

Writing detailed descriptions of intervention plans will take time. Time should be saved in two ways, however: (1) through increased likelihood of success of plans because of their clarity (clients can take copies of plans home with them to refer to as needed); (2) these descriptions together with service agreements can be used in preparing court reports and so save time at this stage, in that it will not be necessary to write lengthy narratives and to cull through lengthy case records for needed information. Also, since some service agreements and plans are identical from case to case within an outcome category, time can be saved by having prepared descriptions that can be filled in as needed.

A service agreement may require amendment for a variety of reasons. Additional objectives may be identified, or changes may occur in an already specified objective. For example, a client who has stated an objective of gaining employment prior to having a child restored may decide instead to apply for an AFDC grant, and the worker may agree that this is an acceptable and possible substitute. Time limits may be reduced (if observation indicates that parent-child interaction is satisfactory and visiting can be accelerated more rapidly than originally planned) or extended (if a parent completes four of five objectives and requests an extension to complete the fifth). Setting additional objectives or changing existing objectives may also necessitate an increase in the original time limits.

When amendments are made, it is not necessary to rewrite the entire contract. A footnote can be added to the original contract, stating which of the objectives has been changed. The footnote should be initialed by all concerned parties, and the original objective being amended can be noted with an asterisk. An attachment describing the change and related plans should be included.

Checklists related to major outcome categories can be helpful in reviewing progress. Each step should be viewed relative to the time within which it is to be accomplished. If both caseworker and client tasks are reviewed in this way and case progress becomes stalled, it is possible to identify both the person who is not fulfilling obligations and the step at which the plan is blocked. Since time is often crucial in providing high quality services, this latter point is of great importance. Such information will be helpful in monitoring critical aspects of casework practice (see examples in later sections). The next section of this chapter provides examples of systematic decision-making procedures within outcome categories involved in protective services for children. You should attend especially to generic characteristics of these procedures.

PRACTICE TASK **3.2**

If your workers use written client-worker service agreements, select a sample of these agreements and review them to determine whether they satisfy the following criteria:

(1) A client-selected goal is stated.
(2) Objectives related to the goal are clearly described.
(3) Intermediate objectives are described.
(4) Responsibilities of clients are described.
(5) Responsibilities of the social worker are described.
(6) A time limit for completion is noted.
(7) Consequences for meeting or not meeting objectives within the time limit are clearly described.
(8) The agreement is signed by all involved parties.
(9) Plans for achieving objectives are clearly described in the agreement or on attachments to this.

EXAMPLE OF DECISION MAKING WITHIN AN OUTCOME CATEGORY

Return of a person from one environment, such as foster care, to another, such as the residence of a child's biological parents, represents an important outcome. Information included in restoration service agreements includes (1) the client's goal (e.g., restoration of a child on a permanent or a trial basis); (2) the worker's agreement to support the parent's goal by making appropriate recommendations to the court if problems are resolved, and by developing intervention programs to help the parents address problems; (3) a description of the potential consequences of nonparticipation by the parent (the objective of having the child returned cannot be recommended to the court and alternative planning must be made); (4) the objectives that must be achieved to attain the goal; (5) the time limits within which objectives are to be accomplished; and (6) the names of involved parties. Plans made to accomplish each objective are attached to the service agreement. These should clearly describe the steps required to achieve each objective. Responsibilities of both the client and the worker should be clearly noted. For example, frequency, place, and duration of parental visits with a child in out-of-home care should be described. It is the worker's responsibility to try to plan initial visits so that they are likely to be successful. This may require brief visits at first. The client's responsibilities for meeting with the social worker should be described. Here, too, we are guided by literature within social work: The frequency with which parents visit their children and the frequency of contact between the worker and parent has been found to be related to achievement of restoration. Thus, two important checks to be made concerning case management procedures concern the duration and frequency of such contacts.

Tasks of the social worker include observation of parent-child interaction during visits as well as agreement to meet with the client on a predetermined schedule. Parents should receive a second and perhaps a third opportunity to attain objectives; but because time is of the essence for children in care, alternative plans should be made following failure of a second or third contract if adequate services have been offered. A case example is presented below. This includes the service agreement used, problem profile formed, and description of plans made to achieve objectives.

THE W. FAMILY: A SYSTEMATIC CASE MANAGEMENT PROCEDURE IN A CASE HEADED FOR RESTORATION

Steven W., 9½ years, was declared a dependent of the court, and criminal charges were filed against his father for abuse. Mrs. W. was not involved in the incident. No court action was taken in regard to the other four children at home.

The first visit with the family took place two days after Steven was placed in emergency care. Both parents said that they wished to have their son returned to their home. The father was not able to recall the sequence of events leading up to the abuse; corporal punishment had not been used extensively in the home and was considered a last resort. Hence the father's abusive behavior was not seen as a typical response.

COLLECTION OF A PROBLEM PROFILE AND PROBLEM SELECTION

During the second interview a problem profile was completed, and the worker and clients agreed to begin working on the first two problems (see Figure 3.1). Reducing the father's drinking was seen as the most important issue by both parents. According to Mrs. W., when Mr. W. drank in the evenings, he retreated from the problems created by the children, which increased Mrs. W.'s responsibilities and frustration. She stated that since she had no free time to herself, her efficiency at home was reduced and she "resented the restrictions on her and the overall responsibility for running the house." Both drinking and frustration in relation to the children's lack of chore completion

Problem No.	Label	Who Labels	Who Has the Problem	Date	Examples	Situation
1	drinking	father	father	5-15	consumes "excessive" amounts of alcohol on a daily basis past history of drinking	at home on work breaks
2	frustration	mother/father	mother/father	5-15	mother assumes all child care and household responsibilities mother has no free time; children will not do chores or follow any instructions (such as to go to bed, to clean up rooms) father becomes angry at children's not complying with requests	all at home
3	criminal charges	father	father	5-15	father charged with 273(d) Penal Code (PC) for abuse	
4	fights with wife's mother	mother	mother	5-15	can't refuse mother's requests	telephone
5	work	father	father	5-15	doesn't like work schedule (hours vary randomly); would like more consistent schedule would like to transfer to a store nearer home	

SOURCE: Stein et al. (1978: 226-227).

Figure 3.1 Problem Profile: W. Family

were considered to be related to the abuse, and assessment efforts focused on these areas. While fighting with her own mother was troublesome, Mrs. W. agreed that this did not occur often enough to give it priority over the first two problems, and the father felt that dealing with problems related to his work could wait until other issues were resolved.

The worker agreed to help Mr. W. resolve the pending criminal charges. The issue of visiting with Steven in the emergency foster home was raised. The boy had been in care for nine days and there had been no visit as yet. The worker stated that he would like to arrange a one-hour visit between Steven and both parents on the following Saturday. While Mr. W. said he was nervous about seeing his son, both he and Mrs. W. said they would like to do this. The worker agreed to speak to the son and foster parents and telephone the parents the next day with a plan for a first visit.

CONTRACTING AND INTERVENTION

The worker spoke to Steven to determine his feelings about returning home. He stated that he would like to return and would like to visit his parents. The visit was observed and went well except for a very brief hesitancy on the part of the father and son to look at and talk with each other. All parties expressed a wish to be together as soon as possible. The worker suggested that a contract be formed with the objective of restoring Steven to his parents' home contingent on reducing the father's drinking and increasing the mother's free time and the children's completion of chores. Since Mr. W. did not show any effects of drinking until after three drinks, it was decided that he could have two drinks per day. Regular visits with Steven were planned (see Figure 3.2).

The parents stated that they could afford five dollars per week to be distributed among the children for chore completion (for details, see Stein et al. 1978). They agreed that Mrs. W.'s free time would be her reinforcer for assisting Mr. W. to decrease his drinking. Mr. W. said that having one hour to himself each day after work would help him to reduce his drinking and that he would like to discuss his job with his wife. Mrs. W. agreed with both suggestions. The worker agreed to discuss Mr. W.'s work with him during their sessions if Mr. W. followed the drinking program. He also agreed to design treatment programs as well as a contract within four days. The worker noted that once progress was observed with the problems in the contract they would consider Mrs. W.'s problems with her mother. The contract is presented in Figure 3.2 and plans in Figures 3.3, 3.4, and 3.5.

This contract is entered into between _____ , child welfare worker for _____ County, and Louise and Stewart W., parents of Steven W., at the present time a dependent of the _____ County Juvenile Court.

In keeping with the wish of both parents to have their son Steven returned to their home on a trial basis, _____ agrees to recommend such a trial visit to the juvenile court, contingent upon the participation of both parents in a program to accomplish the following objectives:

(1) to increase the frequency with which the children in the home complete their household chores (see attached);

(2) to decrease Mr. W.'s alcohol consumption to no more than two drinks per day (see attached);

(3) to increase Mrs. W.'s free time from zero to two hours per week;

(4) to visit with their son Steven according to the attached schedule.

It is understood by both parents that failure to comply with this program will result in a statement to the juvenile court that, in the opinion of the worker, the trial visit is not feasible at the present time.

The contract is in effect for ninety (90) days, beginning _____ and ending _____ .

Signed:

_____   _____
Stewart W. (father)   Worker

_____
Louise W. (mother)

Date: _____

SOURCE: Stein et al. (1978: 231).

Figure 3.2 Contract with W. Family

Regarding the *pending criminal charges against the father,* he was placed on one-year probation with a suspended ninety-day sentence.

Regarding the *mother's fights with her mother,* Mrs. W. stated that her mother telephoned her three or four times a week and made continual requests that she mediate problems she was having with Mrs. W.'s younger brother. A program was designed to help her to decrease these calls. This program included model presentation, behavior rehearsal, feedback, and homework assignments (see Stein et al., 1978). Three weeks form the time the program was begun, Mrs. W. reported

Period covered: three months

First month: (dates)	Saturday afternoon from 1:00 p.m. until 5:00 p.m.
Second two weeks: (dates)	Saturday from 9:30 a.m. until 5:00 p.m.

During the first month, to allow worker observation of the interaction between Steven and his parents, visits should include only the parents and Steven. Mrs. L., who has performed baby-sitting services for the W. family in the past, will stay with the four children during these visiting periods.

Second month: (all visits to occur in the parent's home)

First two weeks: (dates)	Saturday from 9:30 a.m. until 5:00 p.m.
Second two weeks: (dates)	Saturday from 9:30 a.m. until Sunday 5:00 p.m.

Either or both of the parents will pick up Steven at the foster home and return him to the foster home.

Third month:

First two weeks: (dates)	Friday 5:30 p.m. until Sunday 5:00 p.m.
Second two weeks: (dates)	Wednesday 5:30 p.m. until Sunday 5:00 p.m.

Either or both of the parents will pick up Steven at the foster home and return him to the foster home.

If for any reason any of the above visits have to be canceled, either Mr. or Mrs. W. will notify the foster home as much in advance as possible and will telephone the social worker.

The worker agrees to do the following:

(1) Observe at least half of the above visits. The exact time for these observations will vary, but the worker agrees to notify the parents one day in advance.

(2) The worker will observe parent-child interaction in order to identify any problems that may exist. Should any be identified, the worker will discuss them with the parents and will develop a program to resolve them.

(3) If no problem areas requiring extensive intervention are identified, or if any that are identified have been resolved, the worker agrees to request an ex parte order from the juvenile court on _____ . This will permit Steven to remain in his parents' home on a continuing basis beginning _____ , the last visit of this contract period.

(4) The worker will continue to visit the parents' home for a minimum of ninety (90) days following the start of the 90-day trial visit. The objectives of these vists are the same as those noted in item 2.

SOURCE: Stein et al. (1978: 235).

Figure 3.3 Plan for Increased Visiting: Steven W.

The goal of this program is to reduce the number of drinks Mr. W. consumes each day from over six to only two. Mr. W. states that drinking helps him to quench his thirst, and helps him to relax. This program is designed to make drinking of alcoholic beverages contingent upon (1) drinking nonalcoholic beverages to quench his thirst and (2) engaging in other relaxing behaviors while at home.

Before the father may drink an alcoholic beverage, he must first

(1)   quench his thirst by drinking a nonalcoholic beverage such as orange juice, Pepsi-Cola, or lemonade;

(2)   attempt to relax by watching television, reading, or taking a bath.

If he meets those two conditions, he may drink an alcoholic beverage. The number of drinks per day may not exceed two. If Mr. W. complies with this program, he will receive the following:

(1)   After complying with steps 1 and 2, his wife will allow him to discuss his job with her for one-half hour each evening.

(2)   Each day that the father has two drinks or fewer, he will earn one hour of time alone.

The mother agrees to

(1)   have nonalcoholic beverages available in the refrigerator;

(2)   not discuss her husband's job unless he has satisfied steps 1 and 2;

(3)   keep records of time alone that he has earned, and negotiate with him as to when that time will be used.

The social worker agrees to

(1)   monitor the program at his weekly interviews with the parents;

(2)   discuss any problem areas in use of the program and to make alterations if necessary;

(3)   not allow the father to discuss his job unless he has complied with steps 1 and 2 of his program on the day of the interview.

SOURCE: Stein et al. (1978: 233).

Figure 3.4   Plan To Reduce Mr. W.'s Alcohol Consumption

that the phone calls from her mother decreased from three or four per week to two, and that the average length of calls decreased from about thirty minutes to between four and seven minutes. Mrs. W. was pleased with her progress and reported that her mother now seemed more respectful of her.

OUTCOME

Excellent progress was made in three of the four contract areas (see Figures 3.6 and 3.7). Sixty days from the time of contract signing, Mr. W.'s drinking was reduced from a baseline of 6%7 drinks per day to 3½

The desired outcome of this plan is to provide the mother with time alone, as a respite from child care responsibilities and as an opportunity to pursue activities of her own choosing. Time alone will be contingent upon her monitoring Mr. W.'s drinking program. The mother agrees to

(1) have nonalcoholic beverages available in the refrigerator;
(2) keep records of time alone that Mr. W. earns;
(3) allow Mr. W. to discuss his job if he complies with steps 1 and 2 of his drinking program.

If the mother complies with his program, she will earn two hours per week of time alone. The father agrees to

(1) negotiate with Mrs. W as to when she will use her two hours of time alone each week.
(2) be responsible for managing the home, including caring for the children and other household chores during her time alone.

The social worker will review this program at his weekly interviews with the parents and will attempt to facilitate its use and continuation.

SOURCE: Stein et al. (1978: 234).

Figure 3.5 Plan to Increase Mrs. W.'s Free Time

drinks per day. He was earning his one hour of free time and engaging in nightly discussions with Mrs. W. about his work. Mrs. W.'s free time had increased beyond the contract objective of two hours per week to four hours. The parents had negotiated the latter increase on their own, and both were satisfied with this arrangement. Visits with Steven and occurred according to schedule, and no problems were observed by the worker or reported by the parents. The parents still were inconsistent in maintaining records of chore behavior of their children. Information they did collect showed that at the beginning of the program the children were earning an average of four points per day and that this had increased by approximately two points per child per day.

Ninety days from contract signing, Mr. W.'s drinking had decreased to zero drinks per day, and Mrs. W.'s free time had increased to eight hours per week. Mr. W. assumed childcare responsibilities during these additional hours. The parents reported that the children's compliance with household responsibilities increased; however, they did not maintain records in this area. Both parents reported that Mrs. W. had maintained her assertive behavior with her mother during telephone conversations. Two weeks before the end of the contract period, the father was transferred to a new store and was placed on a new work schedule. He had not requested the transfer, although, as indicated on

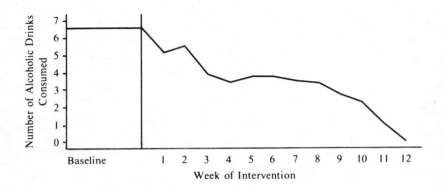

Figure 3.6   Average Number of Alcoholic Drinks Consumed Per Day by Mr. W.

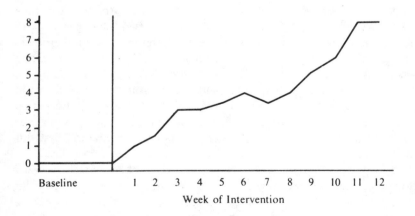

Figure 3.7   Hours of Free Time per Week for Mrs. W.

the profile, he had desired it. Both he and Mrs. W. were very pleased with this change.

RETURN OF STEVEN TO HIS HOME

Steven was returned to his parents' home as specified in the contract. For the first two months following restoration, the worker maintained biweekly in-person contact and alternate-week telephone contact with the family. No problems were observed, nor were any reported by the parents. At the beginning of the third month following restoration, Mrs. W. reported that Steven was beginning to have tantrums (screaming and shouting) and to fight with his younger siblings, although in his father's presence he was said to exhibit exemplary behavior. Mrs. W. was usually in some other part of the house and would become aware of screaming and shouting. She said, "It seemed that the children would get into an argument over toys or what to watch on television and Steven would 'bully' the younger children and, when he could not get his way, would scream and shout."

When asked how she dealt with this problem, Mrs. W. said that she would separate Steven from the four younger children and talk with him about the problem and that she was spending as much as one-half hour to a full hour with Steven each afternoon following these scenes. This greatly distressed her because it interfered with completion of her own chores. She said she knew she was probably supporting this behavior by spending so much time with Steven but that her only concern was putting an end to the yelling and shouting and that this was effective.

Shortly after Steven had been restored to his parents, the worker had suggested that the parents identify some activities, possibly at a neighborhood community center, that the children might engage in after school and on weekends when Mr. W. was working, in order to relieve Mrs. W. of caring for all five children by herself. The parents agreed to contact the neighborhood center and obtain a list of appropriate activities for the children. The worker agreed to meet with the parents and the children in four days to go over the list and to discuss a procedure for enrolling the children at the center. He suggested that, should the problem occur in the meantime, Mrs. W. should not spend time talking with Steven but should use the time-out procedure.

Two days later, Mrs. W. telephoned the worker and told him that she and Mr. W. were convinced that Steven was "hyperactive" and that they had decided to obtain medical consultation. The worker doubted that there was any organic basis for Steven's difficulties but thought that if organicity could be ruled out the parents might be more willing to engage in an appropriate program to eliminate these recent problems. Over the next several weeks, Steven underwent a general physical examination, a glucose tolerance test, an electroencephalogram, a psychiatric assessment, and psychological testing. None of the physical tests indicated any organic problem. The psychiatrist told the parents that he did not believe that psychotherapy was called for and supported the caseworker's recommendation regarding Steven and the younger children.

The parents then followed through with the suggestion that they identify appropriate programs at the community center. Steven subsequently joined the Cub Scouts and enrolled in an arts and crafts class that met twice each week at the center. The worker also suggested that, since Steven enjoyed time with his mother, she should set aside some time each week when she and Steven could spend together sharing a mutually enjoyable activity. Both Steven and Mrs. W. stated that they had always enjoyed reading together and talking about what they read but had never done this on a set schedule. Mrs. W. agreed to spend one-half hour to one hour in this activity with Steven on afternoons when he was not at the community center.

The worker remained with this case for ninety additional days of follow-up, reducing this contact to the biweekly in-person and alternate-week telephone contacts that had been arranged prior to the onset of the last problem. Steven was still reported to fight on occasion with his siblings, but not to an extent that was considered to be a problem. The court dependency was dismissed.

Case management checklists related to return of a child to the biological parents are provided in Figures 3.8 and 3.9. Detailed checklists (see Figure 3.8) can serve as a guide for workers. Abbreviated checklists for all of a worker's cases in a certain outcome category could be completed by each worker on a monthly basis and reviewed by supervisors (see Figure 3.9).

OTHER OUTCOME CATEGORIES

Other outcome categories of concern within child welfare settings include prevention of out-of-home placement (in home protective services), termination of parental rights and subsequent adoption or guardianship (Figure 3.10), long-term foster care with a written agreement (Figure 3.11), and decision making in which the goal is to help clients decide what they would like to do (see Stein et al., 1978).

Yes   *No*

General Questions

_____   _____   A decision to restore the child was made by the parent.

_____   _____   If the child is old enough to participate in planning, he/she is in agreement with this decision.

Problem Selection

_____   _____   A list has been made of problems that must be resolved. The source identifying each one has been noted.

_____   _____   Resolution of problems identified directly concerns the well-being of the child, given that he/she is restored. Useful questions: (1) Will the stability of the restoration be threatened if the problem is unresolved? (2) Would a judge keep this child in care because the parent did not satisfy a certain criterion? (3) If left unchanged, will this harm the child?

_____   _____   Clients understand why each of the problems selected must be resolved.

_____   _____   Clients were involved in problem selection.

_____   _____   Baseline data have been gathered for each problem that will serve as a reference point for evaluating progress (indicate its location).

_____   _____   Baseline data have not been gathered, but a procedure has been described for evaluating progress in each outcome area.

_____   _____   If collateral resources are involved, there is a clear plan for coordinating service delivery and exchanging information.

Service Agreements

_____   _____   There is a written service agreement.

_____   _____   The agreement has been signed by all involved parties.

_____   _____   An agreement has been written, but the client will not sign it.

_____   _____   Clients have been given a copy of the contract whether or not they signed this.

_____   _____   The agreement includes a clearly described schedule for parent-child visits (including time and place), with a plan to accelerate visits.

_____   _____   The visiting schedule is realistic, given the client's current visiting pattern.

_____   _____   There is a plan for ongoing assessment throughout the contract period.

_____   _____   Objectives are clearly described in each area.

SOURCE: Gambrill and Stein (1978: 57-58).

Figure 3.8 Detailed Case Management Checklist for Children Headed for Restoration

(continued)

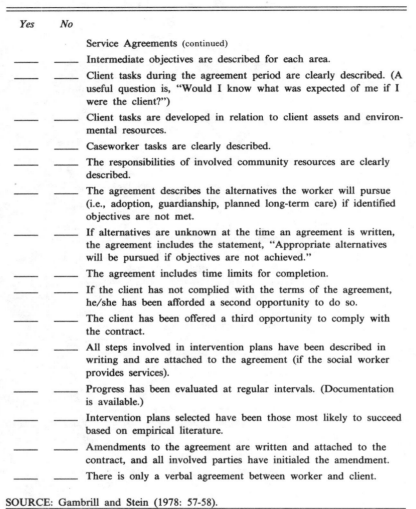

Yes   No

Service Agreements (continued)

_____ _____ Intermediate objectives are described for each area.

_____ _____ Client tasks during the agreement period are clearly described. (A useful question is, "Would I know what was expected of me if I were the client?")

_____ _____ Client tasks are developed in relation to client assets and environmental resources.

_____ _____ Caseworker tasks are clearly described.

_____ _____ The responsibilities of involved community resources are clearly described.

_____ _____ The agreement describes the alternatives the worker will pursue (i.e., adoption, guardianship, planned long-term care) if identified objectives are not met.

_____ _____ If alternatives are unknown at the time an agreement is written, the agreement includes the statement, "Appropriate alternatives will be pursued if objectives are not achieved."

_____ _____ The agreement includes time limits for completion.

_____ _____ If the client has not complied with the terms of the agreement, he/she has been afforded a second opportunity to do so.

_____ _____ The client has been offered a third opportunity to comply with the contract.

_____ _____ All steps involved in intervention plans have been described in writing and are attached to the agreement (if the social worker provides services).

_____ _____ Progress has been evaluated at regular intervals. (Documentation is available.)

_____ _____ Intervention plans selected have been those most likely to succeed based on empirical literature.

_____ _____ Amendments to the agreement are written and attached to the contract, and all involved parties have initialed the amendment.

_____ _____ There is only a verbal agreement between worker and client.

SOURCE: Gambrill and Stein (1978: 57-58).

Figure 3.8 (continued)

Prevention of unnecessary out-of-home placement is recognized as an important goal both in child and adult protective services. The steps involved in offering in-home protective services are almost identical to those involved in offering services where children have been removed from their homes. Clients' participation in decision making is solicited, problems that must be resolved are identified, and protential consequences of client participation or its lack are clearly described in a

Worker _____   Month _____

	Client 1	Client 2	Client 3	Client 4	Client 5
1. Date child entered placement:					
2. Goal determined to be restoration. Date:					
3. Written agreement exists. Date:					
4. Agreement is signed. Date:					
5. Problem areas are identified in the agreement (including their source).					
6. All problems critically relate to return of the child.					
7. A visiting schedule is described in writing in the agreement.					
8. Caseworker and client responsibilities are described in the agreement.					
9. A plan for assessment is included.					
10. Objectives for attaining restoration are clearly described.					
11. Consequences for meeting or not meeting objectives are clearly described.					
12. Appropriate assessment procedures have been completed and are described.					
13. A baseline exists for each identified problem.					
14. Progress indicators for each outcome area have been identified.					
15. Plans for attaining each objective are written and attached to the agreement.					
16. Objectives to be achieved by community resources are described.					

SOURCE: Gambrill and Stein (1978: 59).

Figure 3.9 Case Management Checklist for Children Headed for Restoration

(continued)

	Client 1	Client 2	Client 3	Client 4	Client 5
17. An appropriate process is described for coordination of services.					
18. Amendments are described in writing and attached to the agreement.					
19. Rate and duration of parent/child visits (per week):					
20. Child restored. Date:					
21. Follow-up service plan is written.					
22. Expected date for dismissing dependency:					
23. Dependency dismissed. Date:					
24. Log of contacts with parents is available.					

SOURCE: Gambrill and Stein (1978: 59).

Figure 3.9 (continued)

service agreement. Differences are that in a protective service agreement, a decision has been made to keep the child in the home, and the alternatives the worker will pursue, depending on whether or not identified objectives are met, differ (e.g., the child will remain at home or be placed in out-of-home care). An example of a service agreement for offering in-home services is shown in Figure 3.12. The case management steps involved in helping clients reach a decision are very similar to those involved in offering in-home services and those involved in pursuing restoration.

Cases that start out as restoration cases may end up as terminations of parental rights followed by adoptions, due to clients' failures to follow through with agreed-upon plans. A schedule should be established for following case progress after referral has been made to another source, such as an adoption unit, to ensure that they are moving in a timely fashion. A log, showing referral and acceptance dates, plus worker contacts with sources, should be maintained to substantiate worker efforts in this direction. Here too it may be helpful to ask workers to fill out checklists (see Figure 3.10).

Guardianship, as opposed to adoption, is appropriate as an alternative for children in stable long-term care when the foster parents are not willing to adopt. Cases in which neither restoration nor adoption is

Worker _____   Month _____

	Client 1	Client 2	Client 3	Client 4	Client 5
1. Natural parents (if available) have been informed that such action is being taken.					
2. Section of Civil Code being used:					
3. Attempts to offer services to parents are documented.					
4. Parental response to services offered are documented.					
5. Outcome of any services provided are documented.					
6. Date referred to adoption unit:					
7. Date accepted by adoption unit:					
8. An adoptive home has been identified. Date:					
9. Date referred to county council:					
10. Date accepted by county council:					
11. Frequency of follow-up checks with adoption unit (per week):					
12. Frequency of follow-up checks with county council (per week):					
13. A court date has been set. Date:					

SOURCE: Gambrill and Stein (1978: 71).

Figure 3.10 Case Management Checklist for Children Headed for Termination of Parental Rights and Subsequent Adoption

possible should be reviewed to see if this option is viable. Guardianship has distinct advantages over planned long-term care, since such arrangements afford legal safeguards for the foster parents and the child. This increases the likelihood of continuity of care for children. A disadvantage lies in the absence of guardianship subsidies. Clients may not know what goal they want to pursue. A decision-making agreement can be formed, and casework activity can be directed toward helping clients arrive at a decision. Decision-making agreements differ from

Worker _____   Month _____

	Client 1	Client 2	Client 3	Client 4	Client 5
1. Date child entered placement:					
2. Date categorized long-term care:					
3. Energetic attempts have been made to locate parents (attempts are documented in case file).					
4. Cannot locate parents; there are no grounds for termination.					
5. Parents' whereabouts are known; attempts to engage them in case planning have failed (attempts are documented).					
6. Parent is temporarily unavailable (e.g., in prison); expected release date:					
7. Parents' plans for children following release are described in case file.					
8. Attempts have been made to obtain voluntary relinquishment (documented); reason for refusal is described in case file.					
9. Child is not adoptable (record indicates reasons, who made decision, and date).					
10. Possibility of guardianship has been pursued with all likely persons.					
11. No adult will assume role of legal guardian (reasons for refusal are described in case file).					
12. Planned long-term care with a written arrangement is being pursued (date of expected completion).					
13. A written agreement with _____ and _____ exists (date signed):					
14. A clear verbal agreement between _____ and _____ exists (date):					

SOURCE: Gambrill and Stein (1978: 52).

Figure 3.11   Case Management Checklist for Children in Long-Term Placement

This contract is entered into between _____ , social worker for _____ County, and _____ , parent of _____ .

In keeping with the wishes of _____ and _____ to continue to reside together, the social worker agrees to the following:

(1)   to help the parent(s) and _____ try to resolve any current difficulties related to contact of the family with the protective service unit;

(2)   to arrange a way for all involved parties to determine degree of progress;

(3)   to be present at all arranged meetings with family members;

(4)   to arrange for the involvement of other resources as necessary.

Family members agree to the following:

(1)   to meet with the social worker at prearranged times;

(2)   to permit observation of family exchanges during a portion of these visits;

(3)   to cooperate with the social worker in trying to resolve any identified difficulties.

This contract is in effect for _____ days beginning _____ . Identified problem areas and intervention plans are to be attached to this contract.

Signed:

_____   _____
            Parent

_____   _____
            Parent   Social Worker

_____
            Minor

_____
            Minor

SOURCE: Gambrill and Stein (1978: 176).

Figure 3.12   Counselor-Client Protective Service Agreement

restoration agreements in that the objective is to reach a decision within a certain time period. Possible alternatives and their consequences are noted in writing. Because clients understand that options will be reviewed, an atmosphere is often created in which alternatives can be discussed in a nonthreatening manner. Parents should continue to have contact with their children during this decision-making process, and workers should strive to make such visits a positive experience. In this way, clients have information about themselves and their children that is necessary if informed choices are to be made.

The only valid reason for classifying cases as having no plan, or as undecided, is when a child has been in care for less than one month or if the worker and parents are working toward making a decision within the framework of a decision-making agreement. Since it is important that energetic attempts be made to form a plan in a timely manner, it might be best to review *all* cases with no plan every three weeks. New intake should be reviewed on the same schedule. These cases can be identified from the summary form described in the next section. It is important to encourage parents to visit their children even when plans have not been formed, since restoration to biological parents is related to continued visiting (Fanshel and Shinn, 1978).

PRACTICE TASK 3.3

Identify the decision-making steps involved in the two outcome categories that you think are of most concern in your agency.

KEEPING TRACK OF PLANS MADE FOR CLIENTS

Information about plans made for clients is helpful in identifying potential problem areas, such as cases in which no plans have been made, as well as in balancing caseloads and ensuring that agency priorities are followed. Data could be provided by staff on a monthly basis. A card file of cases color-coded by outcome category would make such data very easy to offer, or this information could be available in a computer printout. More specific information is required to determine if classification is the result of careful planning. If the outcome categories of children remain constant over a three-month period, this may be an indication that planning is not occurring in a timely manner. A summary form allowing notation of plans made for all clients in a child protective service unit is illustrated in Figure 3-13. A completed summary sheet should be informative in several ways. Progress in attaining goals should be reflected by shifts in the number of clients across categories. Percentage of cases in different outcome categories and movement within outcome categories can be compared across units.

Certain cases — such a those in which the goal is restoration or in which children have just entered care — require closer review than others — such as cases headed for planned long-term care or those referred to an adoption unit. One way to approach this task would be to randomly select and review on a routine basis two restoration cases from each worker's caseload, two in which children have just entered care, one termination case, and one in which the goal is to arrange for planned long-term care. All cases in which there is no plan should be reviewed often. Cases could be randomly selected in a number of ways; the monthly caseload of each worker could be examined, and every third case that met one of these criteria could be chosen until the required number was obtained.

PRACTICE TASK 3.4

Do you have the following information about the clients in your unit?

(1) total number of clients;
(2) number and percentage of cases in each worker's caseload with a given outcome selected.

If you are unable to answer the preceding questions,

(1) How long would it take you to get the information?
(2) Would you have to rely on reports from your workers for this information?
(3) Are case records sufficiently up to date to obtain this information if the worker were absent?

Information concerning plans made for all clients in care is also of value in balancing caseloads. Some cases require more work and skill than others. For example, new intake cases require more work and probably more skill than do long-term cases in which maintenance contact is the primary task. Examination of a completed summary sheet may reveal an imbalance in the number or type of cases carried by workers. For example, a worker's caseload may contain a majority of long-term cases, thus precluding assignment of many new cases to her. This may result in punishing workers who have to carry the bulk of new cases assigned to a unit. If such a situation is revealed by a review of summary sheets, rebalancing caseloads may be appropriate. It is true that problems may arise in long-term care and that workers may devote a great deal of attention to these cases. We do raise the question, however, Who should offer such services? If a caseworker states that she is overworked but has mostly long-term care cases, is she offering services that should and can be provided by other agencies?

Date	Worker	Caseload Size		Number of Children in Each Outcome Category										
		Children	Families	Restored		To Be Restored	To Be Referred		Referral Made		Long-Term Care		No Plan	Emancipation
				Dep. Dis.*	Not Dis.		Adopt.	Guard.	Adopt.	Guard.	Perm.	Temp.		

SOURCE: Adapted from Gambrill and Stein (1978: 38).

ABBREVIATIONS: Dep. = dependency; Dis. = dismissed; Adopt. = adoption; Guard. = guardianship; Perm. = permanent; Temp. = temporary.

FIGURE 3.13 Overview of All Cases in Unit

There are other criteria that must be considered in balancing caseloads and in assigning new cases such as the need to offer new workers experience and to match client needs with worker competencies; interest of the worker; nature of the problems presented (their complexity); how visible an error might be; willingness of the supervisor and worker to incur risk; and possible administrative sanctions for supervisory failure (Kadushin, 1976). Agency policy directing that cases be assigned on the basis of geographic location may limit your discretion. When these factors are considered together with the worker's caseload size and the workload that this represents (size itself may not necessarily indicate workload), the complexity of balancing caseloads is highlighted. You must (1) be familiar with the competencies of workers, (2) assess the difficulty of cases, (3) match worker skill levels with complexity of cases, (4) assess the workload represented by each worker's caseload, and (5) identify agency objectives and priorities. You can help workers by accompanying case assignment with a clear description of priorities concerning agency objectives and decision-making procedures to be used. Clear identification of decision making steps to be followed within each category will permit you and your staff to determine the extent to which systematic decision making is used.

PRACTICE TASK 3.5

What criteria do you use to balance caseloads?

SUMMARY

Keeping track of the quality of decision making within major outcome categories is an important supervisory task. Tracking of clients can be facilitated by placing clients in major outcome categories of relevance in your agency. A review of the number of cases in a given outcome category in each worker's caseload will be helpful in setting priorities, tracking cases requiring special vigilance, and balancing caseloads.

An in-depth view of the decision-making procedures employed by staff is possible only if the steps in the process are clearly identified. Detailed review of the timeliness and quality of casework procedures can be facilitated by use of case management checklists related to major outcomes.

Chapter 4

EVALUATING THE QUALITY
OF ASSESSMENT

One important set of decisions social workers must make concerns selection of assessment information and frameworks. Information must be gathered about presenting concerns and related factors. This information is used to identify desired outcomes and how these can be achieved. Decisions must be made about what information to gather, how to gather this, and how to organize information. One of your responsibilities is to review the quality of assessment decisions that are made by line staff. Let's say that information is needed about the quality of a client's parenting skills. The social worker could ask the parent about her skills. She could examine case records to see if they contain any information concerning such skills. The parent could be asked to role play what she would do in specific situations, or the worker might decide to observe interaction between the parent and the children during one or more home visits. The parent could be requested to complete a questionnaire concerning parenting skills. There are thus a number of sources of information that could be used.

Workers have preferences about assessment methods. Some prefer self-report; others rely more on observation. Factors influencing selection of assessment methods include familiarity with methods, knowledge about the advantages and disadvantages of each, personal preference, ability to fulfill the requirements for use of a method, and the theoretical framework used to understand presenting concerns and possible resolutions. For example, social workers who use a social-systems, interpersonal psychoanalytic, transactional, or behavioral view of human behavior would be interested in collecting information about the possible role of significant others as well as information about personal factors. Selection of information to use may be based on sound reasons, such as empirical data about the accuracy of data provided by a particular source of information or constraints imposed by what is feasible. On the other hand, decisions may be based on questionable grounds, such as personal preferences unsupported by empirical information or inaccurate assumptions from a practice theory. What may be offered as an objection to a particular assessment procedure, based on a theoretical perspective, may not follow from the theory. Let's say, for example, that a worker accepts an ego psychology perspective for viewing behavior and feelings. There is nothing within this perspective that supports gathering self-report data only and forgoing other assessment methods such as observation. Social workers often have mistaken beliefs about sources of information. For example, some workers believe that observation of of parent-child interaction is useless since such observation drastically alters natural interaction patterns. This is usually not so. There is variation among social workers regarding the weights that they assign various factors when selecting assessment methods.

SOURCES OF
ASSESSMENT INFORMATION

Social workers often use an overly restrictive range of assessment sources, forgoing some of the most reliable ones, such as direct observation. Sources of information include self-report, self-monitoring, monitoring the behavior of others, analogue measures, observation in real-life settings, and case records. Each offers a different way to sample thought, feelings, behaviors, and related events. An overview of these methods is offered in the following sections, including description of important criteria to consider when reviewing the quality of decisions made.

PRACTICE TASK **4.1**

List some sources of assessment information you would like your workers to use more often.

PRACTICE TASK **4.2**

List some reasons your staff does not use these methods more frequently.

SELF-REPORT

Self-report includes verbal reports during interviews, responses to checklists, personality inventories, and projective tests.

Self-report during interviews. Self-report gathered during interviews is the most widely used assessment procedure in social work. Advantages of this method include ease of collecting information and flexibility in terms of kinds of information gathered. People can be asked about their anticipations for the future, or views about past or current events. Their reports may, of course, not be accurate. The more specific the question, the more likely the answer is to be correct if the person has no reason to hide the truth (Mischel, 1968). Some data can be collected only through verbal reports. This is the case with thoughts, feelings, plans for the future, past events, and private behaviors, such as sexual behaviors. Use of other methods, such as direct observation, may not be feasible, as with infrequent behaviors. Thus the interview is a very flexible source of assessment information. Data concerning a wide range of events can be gathered. Nonverbal behavior and speech patterns are available as additional clues to emotional reactions concerning content discussed. It is important to find out clients' attributions of events and whether they attribute them to external or internal causes, consider them stable or changeable, and refer to general personality dispositions or specific behaviors (Janoff-Bulman, 1979; Weiner et al., 1971). People's attributions of events influence their receptivity to change efforts. Accepting reports as valid assumes that the person is capable of accurately observing and reporting information about behavior, thoughts, and feelings, as well as related factors.

Disadvantages of self-report include the possibility that the person cannot provide the requested information, is not willing to provide it, or presents inaccurate views. Information may not be accessible to a person. Perhaps he forgot some sequence of events. Perhaps he never noted the sequence accurately. People often do not accurately observe the relationship between behavior and environmental events and offer reports based on internal predispositions (see Nisbett and Ross, 1980; Loftus, 1979). A person may not understand the question and so report incorrect information. Inaccurate accounts may be due to embarrassment at a lack of information or fears about the consequences of accurate accounts. Information provided may be influenced by people's perception of how they are expected to behave during interviews with workers (Jenkins and Norman, 1975: 134).

Knowledge about the reliability and validity of verbal reports is helpful in evaluating the accuracy of such reports. Familiarity with sources of bias and error may help to reduce distortions in material that may be obtainable no other way (Evans and Nelson, 1977; see Table 4.1). Questions that should be considered include the following:

(1)   Is client's verbal report an accurate representation of her current construction of the events; i.e., is the client speaking honestly?

(2)   Is the client's current construction of prior events the same as her construction of the events while experiencing them? For instance, although a person may interpret and report a situation accurately and/or rationally during the interview, it is possible that when she is actually *in* the situation her interpretations are inaccurate and/or irrational. This is an important consideration if cognitive construction of an event is considered to be an important determinant of behavior.

(3)   Is the report of events an accurate and complete account of events that occurred (Linehan, 1977: 45)?

TABLE 4.1
Advantages and Disadvantages of Various
Sources of Assessment Information

Source	Characteristic				
	Ease of Use	Accuracy	Flexibility	Detail of Information	Sensitivity
Self-report during interviews	H	L-H	H	M	L-H
Checklists	H	L-H	M	L-M	L-M
Personality inventories	H	L-H	L	L	L
Self-monitoring	M	L-H	H	L-H	L-H
Tape recorders	M	M	M	H	L-H
Monitoring behavior of others	M	L-H	H	M	L-H
Analogue situations	H	L-H	H	H	L-M
Observation by trained staff	L-M	M-H	L-M	H	M-H
Case records	H	L-H	H	L-H	L-H

NOTE: H = High; M = Moderate; L = Low
      *"Sensitivity" refers to the degree to which a measure reflects change that occurs.

Examples of research findings about the accuracy of parental reports illustrate some concerns about self-report data. Parental attitudes, feeling states, and child-rearing practices are not as likely to be accurately reported as factual events in a child's life (Yarrow et al, 1970). Social desirability influences parental reports in terms of "placing the information in a positive light, showing precosity of development, or tending to be in line with socially accepted child-rearing practices" (Evans and Nelson, 1977: 616). Attitudes of parents toward an event, such as anxiety over a new baby, show poor reliability; that is, parents give different reports at different times (Brekstad, 1966). Parental perceptions shift over time in line with cultural stereotypes. One factor that has been found to influence such shifts was the availability of Dr. Spock's book (Robbins, 1963).

Perception of a person's current personality influences recall (Yarrow et al., 1970). Distortions by parents regarding the timing of a problem are often related to popular proposed theoretical causes, such as sibling rivalry; problems are sometimes inaccurately reported as beginning with the birth of the next child. People are able to describe some situations more accurately than others. The emotion associated with an event and a parent's current anxiety influence parental reports. Wenar and Coulter (1962) found that reliability of parental report was poorest concerning attitude toward the problem behavior that had brought them to a clinic a few years earlier. Parents of autistic children showed impaired thinking only when the focus of discussion was on their psychotic child and not when the focus was on their normal children (Schopler and Loftin, 1969). Children's descriptions of their unacceptable behavior is no more accurate than that of adults in similar circumstances (e.g., Hartshone and May, 1928). Children, like adults, often cannot identify factors related to their behavior. Often there are discrepancies between reports of children and those of parents. For instance, Lapouse and Monk (1958) found that agreement between mother and child was only 52 percent of overactivity (denied by the child) and 54 percent on nightmares (the child reported more nightmares).

Very talkative respondents are not as accurate as less talkative ones, especially if they seem not to carefully consider what they will say before speaking. Mothers provide more reliable information than fathers. Identical independent reports from parents are likely to point to accurate information. When individuals indicate that it is hard for them to remember some event, it is likely that their views will not be accurate. Neither social class nor intelligence is related to the reliability of retrospective reports.

Checklists, personality inventories, and projective. measures. Checklists, personality inventories, and projective tests are other forms of self-report. These are more likely to be used by consultants or by the court than by social workers. Social workers should be knowledgeable consumers of such reports. The use of self-report inventories for purposes of assessing problem areas often entails the assumption that the client's report provides measures of some observable events. One problem with such inventories, of course, is that they may not reflect behavior either in past, current, or future settings. There may be no available normative data that allow comparison of a client with other people.

A checklist usually lists a number of more or less specific behaviors and asks the person to respond to each item — for example, to indicate the degree to which each behavior may be a problem. The Behavior Problem Checklist (Quay and Peterson, 1967), for example, lists 88 child behaviors and asks parents to indicate the extent to which each is a problem on a scale from 0 (never a problem) to 2 (often a problem). Items included on the inventory are typically unspecific (e.g., "impertinence").

One disadvantage of checklists is their tendency to emphasize problems rather than resources. (An example of a checklist that focuses on positive behavior can be seen Figure 4.1.) Another disadvantage is the tendency to make use of overall scores to describe a person. This encourages use of "trait" conceptions, which obscure the situational specificity of behavior (Mischel, 1968). For example, responses from checklists have been used to try to identify behavioral clusters. Four different clusters have been derived from the Behavioral Problem Checklist: conduct problems (e.g., disobedience, fighting, and attention seeking), personality problems (e.g., feelings of inferiority, social withdrawal, and anxiety), inadequacy-immaturity, and subcultural (socialized) delinquency. Only to the extent that such behavior clusters may be related to the effectiveness of different intervention procedures is such information useful for case management purposes.

One advantage of checklists is that they may remind respondents about events of concern. A disadvantage is that they may be leading, in that they suggest problems that are really not there. Checklists also are open to sources of error and bias similar to those described in the discussion of verbal reports during interviews. For example, in one study 37 percent of parents indicated that the school attendance of their child had increased when it had actually decreased (Schnelle, 1974). Responses on checklists are subject to the same type of demand characteristics as other self-report data. The term "demand characteristics" refers to pressures in a situation to offer a certain type of report. Thus parents tend to exaggerate the intensity of problems when first

Indicate how well each of the following items describes the parent by circling the appropriate number.

Parent Characteristics	Describes Very Well	Somewhat Descriptive	Not at All Descriptive
Praises child frequently for specific appropriate behaviors	2	1	0
Picks out small behavioral requirements for child that can be accomplished.	2	1	0
Praises accomplishments rather than obedience.	2	1	0
Uses response cost effectively.	2	1	0
Clearly identifies what child is expected to do.	2	1	0
Has age-appropriate expectations for child.	2	1	0
Uses criticism sparingly.	2	1	0
Does not use severe physical punishment.	2	1	0
Eases child into activity changes rather than requiring abrupt changes.	2	1	0
Ignores inappropriate behavior when appropriate.	2	1	0
Offers reinforcers contingent on appropriate behavior.	2	1	0
Avoids mixing punishment with positive consequences.	2	1	0
Uses an appropriate number of rules (not too many; not too few).	2	1	0
Frequently shows physical affection for child.	2	1	0
Encourages independent behavior.	2	1	0
Is receptive to suggestions from worker.	2	1	0
Takes care of child's medical or dental needs.	2	1	0
Feeds child properly.	2	1	0
Helps child with schoolwork.	2	1	0
Has a positive attitude toward child.	2	1	0
Uses instructions effectively (within child's capability range).	2	1	0
Clothes child appropriately.	2	1	0
Arranges for proper supervision of child.	2	1	0
Provides a home that is free of potential physical dangers.	2	1	0
Other (please specify):	2	1	0

Figure 4.1 Behavior Checklist for Parents

bringing their child to a clinic and tend to exaggerate the extent of positive change following a treatment program. This has been called the hello-goodbye effect.

Parents, children, or significant others may be asked to respond to personality inventories, such as Rotter's (1966) locus-of-control scale or the Minnesota Multiphasic Personality Inventory. The stance of practitioners toward such tests has changed over the years from an exaggerated view of the helpfulness of such inventories in terms of case management needs, to an exaggerated negative view, to the more recent view of exploring possible relationships between individual differences as revealed on such tests and effectiveness of treatment.

> Although standardized personality inventories lack the specificity of description of the individual case necessary for behavior change, there is increasing evidence of major trait-treatment interactions that have been largely ignored in child behavior assessment [Evans and Nelson, 1977: 625].

These authors argue that such inventories can be helpful in gross choice of intervention methods and mediators. For example, child aides selected for their "warm, mothering characteristics" were more effective when working with shy-anxious children than when working with children who had acting-out or learning problems (Lorian et al., 1974). Such information should have an influence on the type of mediator employed in similar situations. We have, however, little information of this type. Thus reports based on personality inventories should be viewed with skepticism in terms of their helpfulness in case management.

Projective tests such as the Thematic Apperception Test and the Rorschach were developed as clinical tools largely as a result of conceptualizing projection as a defense. Defensive projection, or the externalization of impulses unacceptable to the ego, is assumed to occur because conscious recognition of these impulses is painful to the ego. Well over 2000 articles have appeared concerning projective tests. Some argue that these indicate that projective tests have such low validity, "that they are of little or no value for individual treatment decisions" (Quay and Werry, 1972: 243). Data obtained from such tests are often more easily obtainable by other methods (see Bernstein and Nietzel, 1980).

PRACTICE TASK **4.3**

List types of errors your workers often make in using self-report.

PRACTICE TASK **4.4**

Describe what you could do to decrease these errors.

SELF-MONITORING

Self-monitoring, in which a person is asked to keep track of some aspect of his behavior and the conditions related to this in the natural environment, is often ignored by social workers as a potential source of information. Other terms for this process are "self-recording" and "self-observation."

Self-monitoring requires the identification of a behavior, thought, or feeling (and events that occur before and after this, if also desired) and the recording of the frequency of its occurrence. Clients may be unable to describe relevant behaviors and situational factors during interviews, and valuable additional information may be gained from data they collect at home. For example, Mr. W. kept track of how many drinks he had each day and the situations in which he drank (see Chapter 3). Rating scales are often used in self-monitoring. For example, a mother could rate her degree of anger toward a child on a scale from 1 (none) to 5 (extremely angry). Cassette tape recorders can be loaned to clients to record relevant interactions at home.

Advantages of self-recording include lack of expense, lack of intrusion by outside observers, and helping people see the relationship between behaviors of concern and other events. A parent may realize that she hardly ever says anything nice to her child but does yell at him frequently. It offers people a useful self-management tool, since accurate observation is a necessary first step toward self-change (Mahoney and Mahoney, 1976). Some events, such as thoughts, can be counted only by self-observation. A potentially abusive mother could monitor her urges to explode and hit her child. This may be a first step in helping her to recognize and control such feelings. Sometimes self-monitoring itself results in positive changes. For example, the daily frequency of positive statements made by a mother to her child increased when these were monitored (Herbert and Baer, 1972).

Whether or not clients will gather information and how representative this will be depends partly on whether a feasible data-gathering procedure is designed and partly on whether the client understands the purpose of monitoring. A recording form should be provided that is easy to use, and clear instructions should be given about what to observe and record, who is to do it, when it is to be done, how it is to be done, where the recording form is to be kept, who has access to the form, what to do if difficulty occurs, how many days' behavior is to be observed and recorded, and when data are to be shared with the social worker. Practice in how to record information should be offered to clients during the interview to make sure that expectations are clear.

Cues may have to be arranged to remind the people to observe and record behavior and incentives arranged to support data collection. Prearranged telephone calls from the social worker to gather data can serve as an important source of support for data collection. Recording must not intrude unduly on other activities. Designing feasible self-monitoring methods is a skill that develops with practice.

Self-monitoring may alter the frequency of behavior. Positive or negative surveillance may be found. Positive effects include the increase in desirable behaviors and decrease in problematic behaviors. For example, students who monitored their study time had higher grades than those who did not (Johnson and White, 1971). Negative surveillance effects are rare and may take the form of increased problematic behavior or a decreased desired behavior.

The effects of self-monitoring usually dissipate over time (Kazdin, 1974). A number of factors influence the reactivity of self-recording — the degree to which recording a behavior alters how often it occurs. One factor is the valence of the behavior being recorded. Self-recording of desirable behaviors often results in an increase in frequency, whereas self-recording of undesirable behaviors may result in a decrease in frequency (Nelson et al., 1975). Another factor is the motivation the person has to change behavior. For example, self-recording decreased smoking only for motivated individuals (Lipinski et al., 1975). Setting performance goals and offering reinforcement for attaining goals increase the reactive effects of self-monitoring (Kazdin, 1974). The nature of the behavior being monitored also influences reactivity, with the monitoring of nonverbal behaviors being more reactive than verbal behaviors (e.g., Peterson et al., 1975).

The timing of self-recording influences reactivity. Behavior that is observed before rather than after the behavior occurs produces greater reactive effects (see, for example, Bellack et al., 1974). The nature of the recording device used, such as a wrist counter or slip of paper, may affect reactivity, since these may function as cues that influence the frequency of behavior (e.g., Maletzky, 1974). Finally, the number of behaviors monitored also may influence reactivity; there will be greater reactivity if one behavior is monitored than when many behaviors are monitored (Hayes and Cavior, 1977).

Self-recording is often inaccurate. For example, agreement between parents' self-recording of their attention to appropriate child behaviors and independent observers' recording of such behaviors were 46 percent and 43 percent, respectively (Herbert and Baer, 1972). Sources of reactivity were noted in the previous discussion. Obtaining a positive surveillance effect is often desirable, and if this is the case, data relevant to enhancing reactivity can be used to good advantage.

If information concerning the naturally occurring frequency of behavior is desired, a number of steps can be taken to increase the accuracy of self-recording. Noting certain behaviors may be aversive and so avoided, such as yelling at children. If possible, a positive alternative should be monitored. Behavior to be recorded should be clearly described and readily identifiable by the client, and a recording form that is easy to use should be available. Recording should be carried out after the behavior occurs, and recording should not be overly intrusive. People will not accurately record information if they are overly busy with a variety of other tasks. Accuracy can be enhanced by arranging for someone else to monitor the same behavior, given that the person is aware of this (e.g., Tokarz and Lawrence, 1974), and by offering reinforcement contingent on accuracy (e.g., Fixen et al., 1972). Adequate training in self-recording is important in increasing accuracy.

The use of tape recorders. Clients may not be willing or able to monitor their behavior, but may be willing and able to record selected exchanges between themselves and significant others on a cassette tape recorder. Tape-recorded sequences compare favorably — in terms of the representativeness of information offered — with data gathered by trained observers in the home (Johnson and Bolstad, 1975).

PRACTICE TASK **4.5**

What percentage of your workers use self-monitoring?

What percentage of opportunities to use self-monitoring do your workers take advantage of?

What beliefs on the part of your staff impede effective use of self-monitoring? Are these accurate?

MONITORING THE BEHAVIOR OF OTHERS

Another way in which assessment information may be gathered is by asking a client to observe and record behaviors of significant others. For examples, a fourteen-year-old boy kept track of the number of times his father refrained from making any comments following a chore the boy completed (Stein et al., 1978). One of the problems between father and son was that the father frequently criticized his son's behavior. Other examples included a wife who kept track of how often her husband took Antabuse, and a husband who monitored his wife's skills in terminating overly long telephone conversations with her mother. Significant others can be asked to gather data describing the behavior of those with whom they interact when these people refuse to monitor their own behavior or when self-recording might offer inaccurate date.

A decision will have to be made whether to inform persons whose behavior is being monitored that they are being observed. Telling them may alter their behavior. Not telling them may raise ethical problems. The concern about whether to inform persons being observed arises when it is important to obtain a representative account of behavior. During intervention, all involved parties should be informed about procedures, including the monitoring of behaviors.

The same factors that may affect accuracy of self-monitoring may affect the accuracy of information noted about the behavior of others. If people know their behavior is being observed there may be a reactive effect, as in self-monitoring. Knowing that you are being observed, either by yourself or by someone else, may function as a cue signaling certain consequences dependent on being observed or the behavior being observed. Knowing that a teenager will note whether or not a parent makes a critical remark following chore completion will probably decrease the likelihood of such remarks. Another effect that may occur is a change in the observer's behavior as a result of observing someone else (e.g., Ciminero et al., 1977). The concern is to obtain a representative account of behavior and surrounding events.

THE USE OF ANALOGUE SITUATIONS

Another source of assessment information is behavior in situations designed to simulate behavior in the natural environment. Analogue situations include (among others) situations in which clients interact together but do so in an artificial environment, such as the office, as well as situations in which clients act out their part in relation to a role played by someone other than real-life participants (such as the social worker). Let's say that a father and son argue, that they can never agree on who is to do what chores around the house. A sample of their interaction can be gathered in the office by asking them to select a topic of concern and to discuss this for ten minutes, trying to arrive at a solution. The client may be asked to role play his behavior with the social worker taking the part of the involved other, such as a teenager.

Advantages of the use of analogues include convenience and efficiency. Information can be gathered without going into the natural environment. Drawbacks include the possibility that behavior seen in artificial situations may not be representative of what occurs in real life (Bellack, 1979). The more similar the analogue situation is to real-life conditions, the more likely behavior will be representative of that in real life.

Analogue situations are useful in assessing child management skills (e.g., Wahler et al., 1965), communication skills of parents and children (Kifer et al., 1974) and couples (Carter and Thomas, 1973), as well as other behaviors, such as heterosexual skills (e.g., Lipton and Nelson, 1980).

OBSERVATION BY TRAINED OBSERVERS IN THE NATURAL ENVIRONMENT

Observation of interaction between clients offers a valuable source of assessment information. Observation can be carried out during visits to clients' homes, schools, playgrounds, or residential settings, dependent upon contexts of concern. The purpose of initial observation periods is to identify behaviors of concern and related factors. Later observation periods may be used to obtain more precise estimates or relevant behaviors. The observed interactions should be checked to determine whether behaviors seen are typical of what usually occurs. For instance, people can be asked whether a given interaction is typical of their usual exchanges.

Advantages of observation in real-life settings include the opportunity to view clients in their natural environments. If other methods, such as self-report, have not supplied needed information, observation in the natural environment offers an alternative method that can be used. Disadvantages of observation include cost and inconvenience, restriction of observed data to overt behavior, intrusiveness of the procedure, and possible reactive effects of observation. That is, being observed may alter interaction patterns. For example, adults show higher rates of positive behaviors with children during direct observation (Baum et al., 1979). Such effects are usually temporary; participants because accustomed to the presence of the observer over observation periods, and interaction becomes more natural. An important point to keep in mind when discussing reactivity is that the purpose of observation is to obtain a representative picture of interaction. Concern arises only if reactive effects are so severe that behaviors viewed were unrepresentative.

Gathering data by observation in the natural environment usually requires training. Decisions must be made about what, when, where, how long, and whom to observe, as well as how to remain unobtrusive. Social workers often overemphasize how much training is required before they can gather useful information concerning interaction. Possible resources for obtaining assistance in observation are often overlooked, such as undergraduate and graduate social work students.

The skill of accurately describing the interaction between clients is a key one, which all social workers should develop to be able to accurately describe the relationships between the behavior of one person and that of another. Let's say that a mother complains that her son is unmanageable. Observation of their interaction may reveal that she ignores her child's appropriate behavior and yells at (and possibly encourages) undesired behaviors. In addition to describing the relationship between behavior and what happens afterward, it is also important to identify events that precede and cue behavior. Only when the mother has ignored many appropriate requests from her child may he then start to yell and scream.

One of the most important skills to develop is to accurately distinguish between what is observed and what is inferred from observation. Although distinguishing between inferences and descriptions sounds easy, often is is not, because of the tendency of workers to make unsupported inferences. After observing interaction between a mother and her son, a social worker may note in the case record that the mother is "hostile" toward the boy. This is an inference from behavior rather than a description of what was seen. Since descriptions of interactions are much closer to what actually occurs, workers should be encouraged to write descriptive accounts. Descriptive information will permit whoever reviews case records (such as a supervisor or a new worker who takes over a case) to gain a more accurate view of behaviors and related events than will general labels such as "hostile," which may be associated with different behavioral referents for different people.

PRACTICE TASK **4.6**

How often do your workers take advantage of opportunities to observe clients and significant others in real-life settings? To determine this, review a random sample of your workers' cases.

PRACTICE TASK **4.7**

Examine a random sample of your workers' cases to determine how often inferences are supported by descriptive data.

THE USE OF CASE RECORDS

Social workers often consult case records to gather assessment information. Possible deficiencies of case records have been noted by many people. For example, Jones (1977) reported that the case records reviewed did not contain any information relative to case planning, nor was it possible to establish that there was any effort made to rehabilitate families or to locate missing parents. A second difficulty concerns the way in which available data are described in case records. A recent report on planning for service delivery stated that the reports relating to social services delivered made it difficult or impossible to describe what services social workers actually provided (Pelton, 1981). Another problem concerns the frequency with which recording occurs. The most recent information in case records may be years old.

In addition to missing or vague information, a further difficulty with case records is the tendency of social workers to focus on pathology rather than on client assets. This will be a disadvantage to social workers who use a "constructional approach" in which goals are pursued through building on client assets (e.g., Schwartz and Goldiamond, 1975; Gambrill, 1983). Some problems with case records are illustrated below in an excerpt from a psychiatric report (Figure 4.2) concerning a twelve-year-old boy. Comments concerning the report are noted on the right. (The numbers in the text at left correspond to critiques on the right).

Case records would be more useful for case management purposes and supervisory review if clear guidelines were established concerning what to record, how to record, and when to record. Guidelines for recording are described in many sections of this book. These should make case recording less burdensome and more valuable to line staff as well as supervisors (see also Tallent, 1976).

PRACTICE TASK **4.8**

Examine a sample of your workers' case records and make a list of positive characteristics of their records.

TEXT	CRITIQUES
"We saw him in our psychiatric clinic on _____ where he was seen by _____ , child psychiatrist. We will not review the extensive history which you sent us, but some of the salient points were the significance of the ordinal position of this boy in the family, who was born late in this marriage, and the caretaking of this boy by the paternal grandmother while the parents both work (3).	(3) Statements are made, singled out as important, but not elaborated on. The reader is left with the impression that there are invidious conclusions to be drawn from these items, that they are pathognomonic signs of some grave disorder, but the reader is offered no guidance as to what the conclusions or illness might be. Nor is the relevance of these statements made clear in the light of any systematic diagnostic hypothesis.
In the interview, Bob did not ever look at the examiner directly. His face was always turned away as if he could not expose himself to a direct confrontation with his problems (4). He revealed his interest in aggressive play, particularly hockey, where one would characterize him as a "dirty player" and where he spends a great deal of time serving penalties (3). His picture of a person shows a light-shaded drawing without hands or feet (3). He describes, and this is supplemented by his mother, some bizarre food habits, which seemed to have been fostered and covertly encouraged by the grandmother (5).	(4) A metaphorical allusion is made — "as if he could not expose himself to a direct confrontation." Rather than being offered as a clarification of a casual hypothesis, it is offered as a cause. No alternatives are cited. No corroborating evidence is cited. No specific situational referents are included. For example, it would seem more important to note that the psychiatric interview occurred at 4:00 p.m. on a day that included a series of medical examinations that were begun at 8:00 a.m., and it would also be important to describe the interviewer's behavior in some detail.
When [his mother] was seen, she confirmed many of our impressions and observations (3). It was especially significant that Bob had done well with his third grade teacher in spelling and reading and usually does well when she tutors him on Thursday night, but then he fails his test on Friday (3). She also told of his concern about eating things that had once been "alive" (3). In summary, we would describe	(5) An allusion is made to "bizarre" behavior but neither the behavior nor its bizarre characteristics are described. Similarly, pathogenic family influences are mentioned but, again, not elaborated.
	(6) The only direct observational evidence offered is that Bob did not look at the psychiatrist, that he

Figure 4.2 Psychiatric Report

(continued)

TEXT	CRITIQUES

Bob as a severe characterological problem, with features of anger and passive-aggressive qualities (6). We feel that whatever might be the perceptual aspects of his problem (7) are minor as compared with the emotional component (8). Our recommendation would be for Bob to be referred for psychotherapy (9) and with the involvement of the parents as well (9).

Thank you for this interesting referral."

plays what the psychiatrist considers to be a dirty game of knock hockey, and that he draws shaded figures with no hands. Nevertheless, Bob has been assigned a far-reaching, highly negative dispositional diagnosis. Despite the fact that this is a diagnosis that would be applicable to virtually every segment of Bob's life, there is no reference made to such areas as peer relationships, family relationships, personal hygiene, and the very broad range of other activities occurring outside of the examination room.

(7) A problem is introduced in the summary without having been mentioned in the text, and no evidence is presented for it.

(8) Emotional problems have not been described but are definitely defined as severe.

(9) No goals are suggested, nor are relevant therapeutic techniques mentioned. It is as though some specific treatment for eating and reading problems would naturally follow from the generalized technology of psychotherapy for characterological problems.

SOURCE: Stuart (1970: 123-124).

Figure 4.2 (continued)

PRACTICE TASK **4.9**

Examine a sample of your workers' case records and make a list of ways in which they could be improved.

IMPORTANT CONSIDERATIONS IN
REVIEWING
ASSESSMENT PROCEDURES

There are a number of points you should consider when reviewing the quality of assessment. One is the importance of using multiple sources of information. Each source has potential inaccuracies; it is therefore wise to use more than one method whenever possible. Self-report data should be supplemented by observation of relevant interactions. Other considerations include the use of a social-systems approach, in which both external and personal factors are considered as these may relate to concerns; a focus on assets and resources rather than on pathology; the extent to which descriptive data rather than inferences are presented; whether information has been gathered concerning actual levels of behaviors, feelings or thoughts of concern; and the reasonableness, parsimony, and usefulness of summary assessment statements (i.e., views of maintaining conditions) made by workers.

A SOCIAL-SYSTEMS APPROACH

Assessment frameworks differ in the extent to which external factors, such as significant others, economic factors, and the community are focused on, as well as internal factors, such as the client's thoughts, feelings, and recall of past events. Social workers differ in the attention they devote to external and internal variables, ranging from one extreme — where only personal factors may be considered — to the other extreme (equally inadequate) — where only external factors are considered, and feelings and thoughts are ignored. A social-systems framework encourages social workers to identify the social systems within which people function in attempting to understand problems and discover solutions, as well as to obtain information concerning related feelings and thoughts. External factors assume special import in social work settings, where clients often have marginal incomes and minimal vocational skills. An example of a systems approach illustrating the many social networks that may influence a child is given in Figure 4.3.

A FOCUS ON ASSETS AND RESOURCES
VERSUS A PATHOLOGICAL APPROACH

Workers differ in the extent to which they focus on client assets and environmental resources as opposed to pathology. The call within social work to start where the client is encourages identification of assets and building on these (e.g., Schwartz and Goldiamond, 1975). Such a view

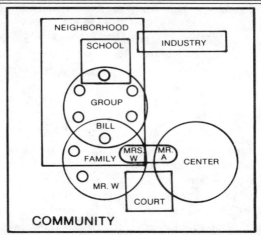

Figure 4.3   A Systems Approach to Assessment

discourages the use of negative labels, which often stigmatize clients and discourage workers unnecessarily from pursuing change. All too often, such labels have no intervention implications (Hobbs, 1975).

INFERENCES SUPPORTED BY DESCRIPTIVE INFORMATION

Material can be reviewed in terms of the extent to which descriptions, rather than inferences, are noted. Let's take two examples of recorded information.

(1)   "This mother has a negative attitude toward her child."

(2)   "On a number of occasions, Mrs. R. scolded her son even when he was playing nicely by himself or playing in a cooperative way (sharing toys) with his older brother. She made many negative statements about him to me, such as 'He is impossible,' and 'He will never change,' as well as directly to her son, such as 'You're always giving me trouble,' and 'You never do anything right.' She did not say one positive thing about her son to me, nor did she praise him once during the entire hour I was with the family."

Statement 2 offers more descriptive information than does statement 1. The latter is a summary statement that may be based on information in statement 2. The descriptive information on which inferences are based should be included in case records. Descriptive data about problems, related factors, and assets will be more helpful than inferences, especially when a new worker takes over a case or a supervisor reviews a case.

ESTIMATES OF INITIAL LEVELS OF BEHAVIORS OR OUTCOMES OF CONCERN

Precise estimates of the severity of a problem are useful for a number of reasons. They offer a more accurate view of severity. Severity may be overestimated or underestimated. An initial estimate also allows more careful evaluation of progress during intervention. Such estimates may be precluded by the time constraints of heavy caseloads or by the need for immediate intervention in crisis situations. Information concerning preintervention levels of a behavior (a baseline) can often be provided by clients or other agencies. Examples of baselines are given below, together with notation of who gathered them.

— Chore completion by children (parents).
— Free time of parent (parents).
— Eye contact between mother and daughter during conversation (social worker).
— Ounces of alcohol consumed daily (father).
— Conversations parent initiates with teenaged daughter during visits (social worker).
— Absence of comments from parent following chore completion by teenager (14 year-old boy).
— Urine tests for heroin use (laboratory).

CLEARLY DEFINED OBJECTIVES

One of the most critical aspects of assessment is identification of desired outcomes. Objectives may be identified by a variety of sources, including the court, the worker the client, or significant others, such as teachers or the police. Selection of desired outcomes may be limited by court mandates that certain changes occur or that certain outcomes be maintained at a given level.

In his book *Goal Analysis*, Mager (1972) refers to vague goals as "fuzzies" and points out that the first important step in identifying specific objectives is to learn to recognize fuzzies. Distinctions must be made between abstract statements and statements that describe actual performances. After a goal is identified, outcomes must be described specifically, so that people will be able to agree that the goal has been achieved. Statements about attitudes are statements of prediction: "No matter what someone says about the attitude of someone else, he is making a prediction about how that person is likely to behave in the future" (Mager, 1972: 15). Thus, if a worker states that a mother has a negative attitude toward her child, she may mean that this mother behaves in certain ways toward her child, such as punishing or ignoring the child's appropriate behavior.

Mager (1972) has identified five steps in the process of goal analysis. Step 1 entails writing down the goal, using whatever words seem reasonable, no matter how vague they may be. A worker may write down "be a better parent." The first important step at this point is to "check the goal to make sure that it describes an *outcome* rather than a *process*, so that you don't get bogged down with the problem of means and ends at the very beginning" (p. 40). For example, if the worker has said "teach the parent better parenting skills," she would be talking about *how* the goal was to be achieved. Confusion of outcomes and how to reach outcomes is a common error when first learning to identify goals.

The second step involves writing down the things you want someone to say or do that would lead you to conclude that they have attained the goal (p. 42). Methods that will be helpful in accomplishing this step include (1) asking what will be accepted as evidence that the goal has been achieved; (2) asking how someone would know if she saw a person who had achieved the goal; (3) identifying someone who represents the goal (e.g., is a good parent) and writing down what he does or says that makes you think this. Mager makes the important point that if you cannot think of anyone who meets your goal, perhaps you are reaching for the unattainable. Achievement of this second step will entail writing down what the person would do or say (the positives) as well as what the person would not do or say (the negatives). For example, perhaps a good parent would

Positives	*Negatives*
take care of child's medical needs	not use severe punishment
feed child properly	not leave child unsupervised
dress child properly	not hit the child
keep the child clean	not allow the child to be abused by husband
be a supportive parent	
provide appropriate play opportunities	
use instructions effectively	

The third step involves going back over your list and, as Mager (1972: 53) indicates, "tidying up" — "there are bound to be a number of fuzzies making their way into your list." There may also be redundancies and items that describe procedures rather than outcomes. Items that describe procedures should be removed from the list, since the objective of goal analysis, or specification of outcomes, is to identify outcomes, *not* to say how to attain them. It should be noted that some goals may be "administrative rather than instructional goals that can only be achieved by an institution, not by an individual" (p. 54). An example of the former would be to decrease absenteeism. An individual goal would be to "have no unexcused absences." Working with the initial list, duplications should be crossed out and abstractions placed on separate pages for further analysis. The first and second steps should be repeated for each abstraction. Grouping of items that have similar meanings may make it easier to sort them.

In carrying out the fourth step, clear statements should be made about exactly what is intended for each performance on the list. For example, in the statement "uses instructions effectively," the word "effectively" may mean one of two things:

(1)   Parent's instructions are clear; that is, the child can identify what the parent would like and when it should be done.

(2)   Parent repeats a clear instruction only once before stating a specific consequence for noncompliance.

In the fifth step the statements identified are tested for their adequacy. "To do this, one asks, If someone performed according to the statements, would you be willing to say that he represents (i.e., has attained) the goal?" Mager, 1972: 66).

A summary of all five steps is shown below (Mager, 1972: 72):

Step 1. Write down the goal.

Step 2. Jot down, in words and phrases, the performance that, if achieved, would cause you to agree the goal is achieved.

Step 3. Sort out the jottings. Delete duplications and unwanted items. Repeat steps 1 and 2 for any remaining abstractions (fuzzies) considered important.

Step 4. Write a complete statement for each performance, describing the nature, quality, or amount you will consider acceptable.

Step 5. Test the statements with the question, If someone achieved or demonstrated each of these performances, would I be willing to say he has achieved the goal? When you can answer yes, the analysis is finished.

PRACTICE TASK **4.10**

Listed below are goals identified by social workers. Check those that are clearly defined. Select ten items that are not clearly defined and give an example of a clear desired outcome related to each.

— Improve parenting skills.
— Child spend overnight visit when visiting with mother; foster parent to accept this.
— Improve housing and financial status.
— Mother regain health.
— Increase homemaking skills.
— Decide which children to return first.
— Make child improve behavior.
— Develop child's strengths.
— Establish parent's visitations on stated regular basis.
— Parents show stability in life-style.
— Improve peer relationships.
— Continued nonuse of drugs.
— Improve housekeeping.
— Improve budgeting.
— Provide transportation.
— Continue court-ordered therapy.
— Parents see psychiatrist.
— Learn nurturing skills.
— Mother to maintain adequate supervision.
— Improve communication.
— Sign up for food stamps.
— Keep away drug-using friends and relatives.
— Keep in touch with son's psychiatrist.
— Reduce sibling rivalry.

Workers often attempt to identify specific objectives in the absence of needed assessment information. If a worker is having difficulty in clearly identifying an objective (for example, how a parent should improve her parenting skills), this should be a clue that more information is needed. Perhaps the worker will have to observe parent-child interaction to clearly define desired changes. It is unfair to clients to impose vague expectations on them — expectations that often the worker cannot clearly define.

ANALYSIS OF MAINTAINING CONDITIONS

Hypotheses or assumptions about factors relating to desired outcomes are made based on assessment information gathered. Criteria of import in reviewing the quality of these assumptions include the extent to which these assumptions (1) are supported by information gathered, (2) point to feasible interventions, (3) take into account empirical information about behavior, (4) consider cultural and ethnic differences, (5) are parsimonious, and (6) can be tested out.

A CHECKLIST FOR VIEWING
THE QUALITY OF ASSESSMENT

You can use the checklist in Figure 4.4 to review the quality of assessment procedures used by your staff. This can also be used by line staff to review their work, as well as to remind workers about important aspects of assessment. When a social worker functions as a case manager, rather than providing direct services himself, assessment tasks are delegated to some other person. In either case, it is important to review the quality of assessment.

PRACTICE TASK **4.11**

Select three cases from each worker's caseload and review these using the criteria noted in the checklist in Figure 4.4.

PRACTICE TASK **4.12**

List below types of errors your workers tend to make when they organize assessment information.

Worker _____ Date _____ Case _____
Number of outcome areas _____   Number directly related to goal _____

a.	Inferences are supported by descriptive data.	1	2	3	4	5
b.	Self-report is supplemented by observations.	1	2	3	4	5
c.	Client assets are noted.	1	2	3	4	5
d.	Negative labels are avoided.	1	2	3	4	5
e.	Sources of assessment information are noted.	1	2	3	4	5
f.	Environmental resources are noted.	1	2	3	4	5
g.	Environmental as well as personal factors are noted.	1	2	3	4	5
h.	Quantitative measures of desired outcomes are available and their location is noted.	1	2	3	4	5
i.	Objectives are clearly defined.	1	2	3	4	5
j.	Analysis of maintaining conditions points to feasible interventions.	1	2	3	4	5

NOTE: 1 = not at all, none (or none available in item h), to
      5 = in all outcome areas.

Figure 4.4   Checklist for Reviewing Assessment Procedures

PRACTICE TASK **4.13**

Describe how each of the errors you mentioned in Practice Task 4.12 could be decreased in frequency. (Refer to Chapter 7 as necessary.)

PRACTICE TASK **4.14**

List positive incentives your workers receive for carrying out high quality assessment.

      They receive: From:

SUMMARY

A variety of sources of assessment information are available, some of which, such as observation in the natural environment and self-monitoring by clients, are often neglected by social workers. Social workers use self-reports of clients in interviews more frequently than any other source of information. Knowledge about sources of bias and error in self-reports should help workers to weigh the value of such data more carefully and encourage them to supplement self report with other sources of information, such as observation during role-played interaction. Checklists, personality inventories, and projective methods often share the disadvantages of a focus on client pathology with a subsequent neglect of client assets, and encourage descriptions of behavior in terms of traits, which usually neglect variations in behavior in different situations.

Each assessment method has disadvantages as well as advantages. Multiple sources should be used whenever possible, to increase the probability of obtaining accurate information. When reviewing assessment methods, it is important to determine the range of sources used, as well as whether weak or strong methods were used — that is, methods that are likely to offer accurate information or methods which are likely to offer inaccurate data. Other items to check include (1) the extent to which inferences are supported by detailed descriptions; (2) the extent to which assets and environmental resources are focused on; (3) the extent to which external as well as internal factors related to problems are noted; (4) whether sources of assessment information used are clearly noted; (5) whether desired outcomes are clearly defined; (6) whether quantitative measures of behaviors of concern are available; and (7) the extent to which negative labels are avoided. It may not be possible to review assessment procedures in all cases on a unit. In lieu of this, probes can be used in which a sample of cases from each worker's caseload is randomly selected for detailed review.

Chapter 5

EVALUATING THE QUALITY OF DECISIONS MADE CONCERNING INTERVENTION

Another important set of decisions social workers have to make concerns selection of intervention methods. Criteria that should be considered are noted in Figure 5.1. This checklist can be used to review the quality of intervention plans and as a reminder to staff of important characteristics of plans. Information required to complete all parts of this checklist may not be available. For example, little may be known about the effectiveness of different procedures in achieving an outcome.

As information accumulates concerning what plan works best with what client, we will be in a better position to determine the possible utility of given plans. However, advantage should be taken of what is known. Let's say that a worker's goal is to increase a parent's effective use of instructions to her child as one attempt to decrease physical punishment. Discussion of new ways of offering instructions will not be as effective as supplementing discussion with model presentation and rehearsal of new skills. As information accumulates, checklists of critical components of given procedures can be designed to remind workers of these as well as to review the quality of their work.

PRACTICE TASK **5.1**

List some criteria you use to evaluate the quality of intervention plans used by your staff.

Worker	Date				
			Client		
	1	*2*	*3*	*4*	*5*

Acceptability to involved parties

Clarity of description

Intermediate steps are described

Feasibility of plans

Likelihood of success based on literature

Efficiency of plan

Likelihood of generalization and
  maintenance

Likelihood of positive side effects

Likelihood of negative side effects

Relationship to assessment information

Separate plans for each involved person
  (as needed)

Description of feasible relevant methods
  for evaluating progress

NOTE: Points could be awarded in each area ranging from 1 (the lowest rating)
to 3 (the highest rating). Overall rating on a case could range from 12 to
36.

**Figure 5.1   Checklist for Evaluating the Quality of Intervention
Plans**

PRACTICE TASK 5.2

Use the checklist in Figure 5.1 to review a sample of cases. You can
use this information to find out what your workers do well, and
where further training or prompting may be required.

MAJOR INTERVENTION ROLES

A review of major intervention roles is helpful in identifying
advantages and disadvantages of each. Four major roles exist: the
verbal method, instigation, replication, and direct intervention (Kanfer
and Phillips, 1969). Each has advantages and disadvantages that should
be considered not only when offering direct service but also when
selecting an agency for a referral.

THE VERBAL METHOD

In the verbal method, reliance is placed on the verbal interaction between the social worker and client. This is one of the most widely used modes of intervention within social work. Requirements include verbal facility on the part of the client and the ability of the client to employ insights to alter behavior, thoughts, or feelings in real-life settings. The approach assumes that people possess requisite skills for translating insight into overt action. Through discussion, the client may form more helpful conceptualizations of concerns, decide what she would like to do in a situation, and acquire more effective problem-solving skills. The support provided to clients is a very important outcome of the verbal method as well as of the other intervention roles. The focus in the verbal role is mainly on the client. Skills required for this method lie primarily in the area of interpersonal competencies, Generalization and maintenance of effects is problematic, since intervention does not take place in the natural environment (see Chapter 10). Verbal exchange is also an important aspect of instigation. Interpersonal skills are important in both the verbal and instigative modes of intervention.

INSTIGATION

This intervention mode also depends on verbal communication between social workers and clients and on mediational processes that bridge the gap between the interview and real-life settings. The interview is the context for both the verbal and instigative modes. The focus in instigation is on behaviors that occur *outside* of the interview in real-life settings. The prime characteristic of the instigative method is the use of agreed-upon assignments that the client carries out in the natural environment; an instigation is an instruction given in one context that is to be carried out in another. Examples of assignments are given below.

Recording Assignments

— Keep track of free time accumulated.
— Keep track of chores completed.
— Record ounces of alcohol consumed daily.

Intervention Agreements

— Respond to first request a child makes.
— Enroll children in nursery school by _____ (date).

— Arrange for day-care for children between time they arrive home from school until parent returns (i.e., locate a day-care center and make arrangements to enroll child).

Generalization and maintenance are not as problematic as in the verbal role, since changes occur in the natural environment. Since such changes must be mediated by clients, their cooperation is important in completing assignments and sharing results, and the client must possess required skill and comfort levels to carry out assignments. Successful task completion can be facilitated by skill of the social worker in arranging reinforcement for assignment completion and in selecting assignments that are within the skill and comfort capabilities of clients. An advantage of the instigation mode is that a range of behaviors can be addressed, including behaviors that are private and that are associated with events that are not available to the social worker. Next to the verbal method, the instigative mode of intervention is the most frequently used role in social work.

REPLICATION

A third intervention mode involves alteration of behavior, thoughts, or feelings in simulated or role-played situations. A parent and her teenage son may practice new ways of problem-solving in the office; or a client may learn how to relax in the presence of imagined, anxiety-provoking events in the office. A parent may practice new ways of praising his child for appropriate behavior and ignoring negative behaviors. Advantages of replication include the following: Practice in a simulated setting is a step closer to real-life events than simply speaking about these events; new behaviors can be practiced in a safe environment; fewer verbal skills are required; constructive feedback can be immediately offered, and client skill and comfort can be more accurately assessed compared to verbal methods alone. Disadvantages include the possibility that behavior observed may not be representative of that in real life. Since behaviors are practiced in artificial contexts, such as the agency, arrangements must be made to make sure they occur in the natural environment. Examples of replication: (1) Teenagers and their parents learn more effective ways to resolve conflicts (Kifer et al., 1974); (2) clients learn more effective employment interview skills via role playing (Gillen and Heimberg, 1980).

DIRECT INTERVENTION

This mode of intervention involves working in the natural environment. For example, the social worker could cue a parent on how to react to her child during exchanges that occur at home. Thus, in this intervention method, the worker enters the natural environment of the client and actively influences behavior in the environment. There is less concern about generalization since work occurs in the natural environment. Fewer verbal skills are required. Disadvantages include time involved in visiting real-life settings and the possible intrusiveness of the worker.

PRACTICE TASK 5.3

Of the four major types of intervention discussed, which ones would you like your workers to use more frequently?

Describe what you could do to encourage your staff to use these more frequently. (Consult Chapter 7.)

THE IMPORTANCE OF
INTERMEDIATE STEPS

Intermediate steps will often be required to attain an objective. For example, many steps will be required to relocate in a new type of housing or to establish more effective child management skills. Intermediate steps should build upon client assets. Information concerning relevant skills should be collected during assessment. Initial skill levels, desired outcomes, and intermediate steps should be clearly described. Identification of steps that lie between initial skill levels and desired objectives compose an agenda that offers guidelines for selecting next steps. Initial steps pursued should match client assets and environmental opportunities. They should consist of the closest approximation to a desired outcome that is achievable and comfortable for clients. Let's assume that an objective is for a client to participate in activities offered by a neighborhood center two evenings a week. Intermediate steps and related skills may be as follows:

Available Assets	Subgoals
1. Mrs. R. has access to a phone and has required telephone skills (what questions to ask; what information to offer).	1. Mrs. R. will telephone the _____ social center no later than Tuesday of _____ and request that information regarding center activities be mailed to her.
2. Same as above regarding telephone skills, and Mrs. R. does have greater interests in some activities than others.	2. Mrs. R. will select from the brochure one activity of interest to her and telephone the center director no later than _____ to arrange an appointment to discuss her possible participation.

Simply telling Mrs. R. to participate in center activities twice each week would result in failure if she does not have required skills. For example, she may not know how to initiate conversations or feel very uncomfortable entering a room full of strangers. Another example of identifying intermediate steps and assets is given in the next section.

Example: employment. The client has work skills as a printing-press operator and as a warehouseman. Let us assume that he wishes to work as a printing press operator, and the goal is to obtain full-time employment as a printing-press operator within thirty days.

Available Assets	Subgoals for Next Three Weeks
1. He knows where the employment office is and can fill out required forms.	1. Register at the state unemployment office.
2. He can identify relevant agencies and complete required forms and interviews.	2. Register with two employment agencies in the city.

3. He has access to a newspaper and knows where to look for printing-press-operator jobs.

3. Review the newspaper want ads daily, specifically looking for job advertisements as a printing-press operator.

4. He has adequate telephone skills and needed interview skills and can manage his behavior to meet commitments.

4. For any jobs that are identified through the above channels, Mr. I. will make and keep appointments for interviews.

Intermediate steps and available assets can be written down on weekly assignment sheets. Progress achieved with initial steps provides information as to what next steps should be. Weekly assignment sheets describing the client's current relevant skills and the intermediate steps selected for that week can be used to clarify agreements concerning objectives, emphasize client assets, and provide a record of weekly progress (Schwartz and Goldiamond, 1975). Responsibilities of the social worker should be included on weekly worksheets. In the above example, one task would be to assist Mr. I. in resolving any difficulties encountered.

PRACTICE TASK 5.4

List the intermediate steps that might be required to encourage an older person to visit a senior center each week.

One of the most common reasons for failure to meet intermediate objectives is that the steps agreed on were too difficult for the client. You should encourage your staff to help clients select achievable steps that are directly related to their desired outcomes. If intermediate steps are not achieved, possible obstacles should be explored. A first question to raise is whether the assignment was carried out as agreed on. If not, the reasons for this should be explored. Perhaps instructions were not clear, or the client did not understand the relationship of the step to achievement of his outcomes. Perhaps no positive incentives were arranged for task completion. Reviewing procedures and rationales for these will be helpful in identifying unexpressed objections and unanticipated obstacles (see Gambrill, 1983; Pinkston et al., (1982). Clients should be encouraged to gradually assume more responsibility for identifying intermediate steps and programs to achieve them. This can be done by asking them to complete a weekly worksheet in which next steps and their relationship to desired outcomes are described (Schwartz and Goldiamond, 1975). This serves as a check that subgoals are clearly related to agreed-up on objectives.

PRACTICE TASK **5.5**

Review a sample of cases to determine what types of errors your staff make in relation to identifying appropriate intermediate steps.

DESCRIPTION OF PLANS
MADE AND IMPLEMENTED

Often, when we turn to case records we find that it is impossible to find out what was done. Terms such as "supportive casework" or "psychotherapy" do not tell us what the social worker actually did. A helpful question to ask when evaluating the clarity with which plans are described is whether there is sufficient description to allow you to replicate what the worker did. We need to know what the worker did, when she did it, how often it occurred, and toward what objective it was addressed. Documentation of service efforts is very important. Only if supportive documentation exists can cases be built in court to support positions recommended by social workers, such as termination of parental rights. The need for this has been stressed by others as well. For example, Pike et al. (1977: 40) include the following quote from a supervisor: "A primary essential, unavoidable rule is *document, document, document*. . . . Proper recording of the worker's activities is directly related to success in court." Social workers often fail to keep careful track of their service efforts and are then in the frustrating position of wishing to pursue a course of action but not having evidence to support this action. If plans related to each problem area are described on separate sheets, these will be readily available for reference (see Chapter 3).

PRACTICE TASK **5.6**

Review a sample of case records written by your staff and identify three ways in which description of intervention plans could be improved.

EVALUATING PROGRESS

The proof of the pudding in terms of the effectiveness of intervention is whether desired results are achieved. Does insight-oriented counseling decrease the probability that a parent will abuse her child again? Does a parent-effectiveness training course increase a parent's skills in interacting with his fourteen-year-old daughter? Desired outcomes must be clearly identified in order to answer such questions, and progress indicators must be selected and monitored. Sources used to gather assessment information may also be used to evaluate progress. Problems in using self-report measures to assess progress have already been noted, for example, the tendency to report greater positive changes than have occurred (see Chapter 4). Other methods that could be used include self-monitoring, role playing, and observation. Examples of measures used to evaluate progress are shown below. In each instance the quantity, frequency, duration, or percentage of some relevant measure before intervention (i.e., during baseline) was compared with the quantity, frequency, duration, or percentage during intervention.

— ounces of alcohol consumed each day
— number of drug-free days
— number and duration of positive conversations
— percentage of chores completed each day
— percentage of days on which a "clean urine test" was found
— number of enjoyable conversations each day
— percentage of conversations between a parent and her teenage son in which the parent asked her son a question about his day
— percentage of nights a youngster met curfew time

Rate of change must be used as a measure when observation times differ in length. For example, perhaps a mother observed her child's behavior for thirty minutes one day and twenty minutes the next. To find the rate of behavior she would divide number of minutes into the number of behaviors she recorded each day. The use of rate as a measure permits comparison of behavior over different time periods. Examples are shown below.

— rate of participation of group members
— rate of instructions followed
— rate of positive comments between a couple
— rate of childcare activities carried out by staff

SCALE ATTAINMENT LEVELS	SCALE 1: Employment (interest in work) self-report ($w^1 = 10$)	SCALE 2: Self-concept (physical appearance) patient interview ($w^2 = 15$)	SCALE 3: Interpersonal relationships in training program, as judged by receptionist. ($w^3 = 5$)	SCALE 4: Interpersonal relationships; report of client's spouse ($w^4 = 8$)
a. Most unfavorable outcome thought likely:	Client states he does not want to work or train for work.	(1) Has buttons missing from clothes, (2) unshaven (says he is growing a beard, (3) dirty fingernails, (4) shoes unshined (if wearing shoes needing shine), (5) socks don't match.	Never spontaneously talks to anyone; may answer if spoken to.	No friends and no close friends (i.e., friends with whom he can talk about serious, intimate topics and whom he feels like his company).
b. Less than expected success:	Client states that he may want to work "some day" (a year or more later) but not now; wants no training.	4 of the above 5 conditions.	Spontaneously talks to his own therapists or caseworkers, but to no other clients.	One person who is a friend or acquaintance but not a close friend.
c. Expected level of success:	Client states that he might be interested in working within the next 12 months, but only if no training is required.	3 of the above 5 conditions.	Spontaneously talks to therapists, case workers, and one other client.	Two or more persons who are friends, but not close friends.

SCALE ATTAINMENT LEVELS	SCALE 1: Employment (interest in work) self-report (w^1 = 10)	SCALE 2: Self-concept (physical appearance) patient interview (w^2 = 15)	SCALE 3: Interpersonal relationships in training program, as judged by receptionist. (w^3 = 5)	SCALE 4: Interpersonal relationships; report of client's spouse (w^4 = 8)
d. More than expected success:	Client states he might be interested in working within the next 12 months, and training for no more than 30 work days.	2 of the above 5 conditions.	Spontaneously talks to therapists, case workers, and 2 to 4 other clients.	One close friend, but no other friends.
e. Most favorable outcome thought likely:	Client states he might be interested in working within the next 12 months; will train for as long as necessary.	1 of the above 5 conditions.	Spontaneously talks to therapists, case workers, and 5 or more other clients.	One or more close friends, plus one or more other friends or acquaintances.

SOURCE: T. J. Kiresuk and G. Garwick, "Basic Goal Attainment Scaling Procedures," pp.338-401 in *Social Work Processes*, edited by B. R. Compton and B. Galway. Copyright © 1975 by Dorsey Press. Reprinted by permission.

Figure 5.2 Example of a Goal Attainment Follow-up Guide

Changes can be plotted on graphs for easy inspection. Graphs offer clear presentations of progress (as can be seen in Chapter 3). One purpose of case records is to indicate degree of progress. In traditional forms of recording, results related to a given area are often mixed with other material, requiring a search through lengthy records to cull out information. Progress can be more readily and clearly seen by keeping track of results over time on forms and graphs designed especially for this. These forms and graphs can be attached to court reports, used for supervisory review, and reviewed by clients and workers when deciding upon next steps.

Goal-attainment scaling offers another way to assess progress. This procedure involves identifying a series of objectives in terms of desirability. Goal-attainment scaling was originally developed for use in community mental health programs (Kiresuk and Sherman, 1968). The first step is identification of major areas in which change is desired. For example, in the illustration in Figure 5.2, four areas are identified: employment, self-concept, interpersonal relationships in training programs, and interpersonal relationships in friendship networks. The overall time frame involved is usually six months. If desired, each problem area can be given a weight to indicate its relative importance. (Weights are indicated in Figure 5.2 by the numbers following the small w's.) Sources of information used are noted in the title section of each scale.

A second step involves selection of a variable in each area that will serve as a measure of success. For example, in Figure 5.2, interest in work will be assessed in terms of specific client statements in relation to work. A third step requires the identification of a series of outcome levels in each area based on the variables selected in the second step. The expected level of outcome should be the one considered most likely, and outcomes that represent more and less than expected are included above and below the expected outcome. Progress can be assessed in terms of outcomes attained, arriving at a "goal attainment change score" (Kiresuk and Garwick, 1975: 394). Baseline levels can be indicated on the scale by placing an asterisk in the cell corresponding to this value.

Helping staff to develop *useful* evaluation skills is one of your most important tasks. It is important not only for accountability to clients but also for your own work satisfaction, as well as satisfaction that staff receive from their work. Development of evaluation skills will usually require training in how to define clear goals, objectives, and progress indicators. You cannot rely on graduate programs to train social workers in such skills. If workers understand the relationship between evaluation of progress and case planning, they are more likely to carefully evaluate progress.

Evaluation allows workers to make important case planning decisions, such as when to remove an intervention because objectives have been achieved and when to select another intervention because no progress has been made. You will have to help your workers select evaluation measures that are relevant and feasible. For example, rather than monitoring behaviors weekly, such a conflict-resolution skills among family members, probes could be used before and after training and at a one-month follow-up during role plays in the office. In addition, clients could be asked to evaluate the quality of their conflict-resolution skills on a scale ranging from 1 (very poor) to 5 (very good) before and after intervention and at follow-up. This will offer both objective and subjective information concerning progress. Both kinds of information are important. Self-reports of change, or its lack, provide information about social validity — that is, whether consumers view services as helpful.

As with all skills, it will be important not to overload workers with new material and expectations and to start where they are in terms of competency level. They could for example, apply new evaluation skills to only one of their cases. See other sources for detailed description of evaluation methods (e.g., Bloom and Fisher, 1982; Gottman and Lieblum, 1974; Jayaratne and Levy, 1979).

PRACTICE TASK 5.7

List some methods typically used by your staff to evaluate progress.

PRACTICE TASK 5.8

What methods of evaluation would you like your staff to use more often?

A PROCEDURE FOR EVALUATING THE CASEWORK PROCESS

You can rapidly evaluate a selected number of cases along a few key dimensions using products generated by a worker in cases in which direct services are offered by workers. For example, a case record can be scanned to determine whether or not the following are present: (1) an identified goal and anticipated date of accomplishment; (2) a written-client service agreement; (3) clearly described objectives, including intermediate ones; (4) baseline measures; (5) a log of worker-client contacts; (6) clearly described intervention plans; and (7) data permitting evaluation of progress for each outcome area (see Figure 5.3). Evaluation of process based on written products is used routinely in some community mental health centers (Rinn and Vernon, 1975; Bolin and Kivens, 1974; Rossi, 1982).

	Possible Points	Client 1	Client 2	Client 3	Client 4	Client 5
Social Worker _____ Month _____						
1. A goal is identified, as well as the expected date of accomplishment.						
2. A written client-worker service agreement is available						
3. Objectives are clearly described, including intermediate ones.						
4. Baseline measures are available.						
5. A log of client-worker contracts is available.						
6. Intervention plans are clearly described.						
7. Relevant data describing degree of progress in each outcome area are available.						

Figure 5.3   A Brief Checklist for Evaluating Casework Process

SUMMARY

A review of the quality of intervention procedures used is important, whether services are provided by in-house staff or by outside resources. Important dimensions to consider when assessing intervention plans include clarity of description, feasibility, likelihood of success, cost, discomfort involved, efficiency, likelihood of generalization and maintenance, and likelihood of positive and negative side effects. An informed decision concerning the adequacy of plans can be made only if these are clearly described and if data are available permitting evaluation of progress.

Chapter 6

COORDINATING SERVICES

Methods to coordinate the services of all parties involved in a case are essential to effective case management. Involved resources may include services external to your agency, such as psychiatrists, psychologists, drug and alcohol treatment programs, day-care centers and public health officials, as well as those provided by other units in your agency or department. Obstacles to coordination include a lack of trust between different professional groups, concern that sharing case material — a necessary component of coordination — will violate client confidentiality; a negative view of clients that may interfere with effective service delivery; and failure of administration to assume responsibility for developing procedures to resolve these problems (see, e.g., Weinrich, et al., 1977; Hobbs, 1975; Helfer and Schmidt, 1976).

If the tasks of each party involved in service delivery are not clearly described and if there is no consensus regarding case goals and methods to evaluate progress, attainment of desired outcomes will be difficult if not impossible. Without planned coordination, the services provided by different resources may be counterproductive. Each social worker may have his own agenda and work within his own time frame. Since assessment and treatment methodologies, as well as objectives, vary across different schools of therapy, the result may be an aggravation, rather than a resolution, of a client's difficulties (Madison, 1977). Unless there is an explicit understanding of the respective responsibilities of each party involved, service delivery may proceed on inaccurate assumptions regarding what each person is doing. A resource person may fail to gather data required to evaluate progress (Madison, 1977). Information required for court reports may not be exchanged without prior agreement to do so.

PRACTICE TASK **6.1**

List three procedures your workers use to coordinate services.

PRACTICE TASK **6.2**

List two procedures your staff should use to coordinate services but do not.

Few models are available to serve as guides for coordination of services (see for example, Polansky et al., 1975; Madison, 1977; Temporary State Commission on Child Welfare, 1976; Public Services Administration, 1973). Recommendations made are often global, such as the suggestion to locate all services within a single multipurpose agency (Kenniston and Carnegie Council, 1977; Advisory Committee on Child Development, 1976: 94). Exactly how this will resolve difficulties created by the absence of a coordinating framework is not clear. Protective services, foster home placement, and adoption units in public welfare agencies are frequently located in one physical plant; however, problems in coordinating services across these units often occur (Office of Program Evaluation, 1977). The use of contracts between agencies has also been suggested (Helfer and Schmidt, 1976). In this context, the concept of contractual relationships refers to purchase-of-service agreements that specify conditions for the use of services, such as foster home placement made by a private welfare agency (Office of Human Development, 1976). While important in terms of arranging resources, the critical problem of coordinating services on a case-by-case basis is not necessarily addressed by such agreements. The responsibility of administrative staff to develop guidelines for service coordination has also been noted (Weinrich et al., 1977). Certainly administrative leadership is essential. However, guidelines will not be useful unless they include *specific* recommendations.

Our main concern here is with coordinating external resources. This is not to minimize the importance of the coordination of intra-agency resources. A great deal of time may be saved by early involvement of intradepartmental staff. For example, case objectives will be more readily attainable when a protective service worker involves a placement worker in his case if it seems out-of-home placement of a child is likely. Natural parents may be most accessible prior to removal of their children. Many parents have to relocate after a child is placed in foster care, since many lose their AFDC grants. Future planning for a child should begin prior to removal. Problems in need of resolution if the child is to be returned are best assessed while the family unit is intact. After placement, assessment must take place under artificial conditions; that is, parent-child interaction is generally observed in environments other than those to which a child will return. Developing case plans and written service agreements between clients and social workers prior to removal encourages a sense of active involvement on the part of clients in the planning process and enhances the likelihood of their continued involvement.

Likewise, placement workers should begin consulting with adoption staff as soon as it appears that adoption may be a case outcome. Exploring whether there are grounds to sustain a termination petition by early involvement of adoption staff may provide essential information regarding the likelihood of this outcome. Timely decision making and exploration of alternatives will increase the quality of services offered to clients.

REQUISITES FOR
COORDINATION OF SERVICES

The goals of coordination are to arrange for and monitor the delivery of all services deemed essential to accomplish a case plan; to provide these services in a timely manner; to avoid duplication of services; and to collect, summarize, and report data regarding degree of progress. Availability of resources will influence options for coordination, and the steps described below may have to be modified if there is a lack of resources. Also, court orders mandating specific types of services may constrain selection of collateral services.

The worker's first task is to complete assessment including identification or desired outcomes. She must then decided what her role will be in the case: Will she provide services in certain areas, soliciting collateral support in others; or will she function as case manager, delegating all responsibilities to other resources? Personal competencies of workers and time constraints are major determinants in making this decision. Once a decision has been made, the following criteria should be considered when selecting resources: (1) The worker should be familiar with the problem-solving approach used by any resource person whose aid she will solicit and with the demonstrated effectiveness of that approach for resolving the specific problem at hand; (2) the collateral must agree to give priority to problem areas for which he was brought into the case; (3) the collateral must agree that he can work on the problem within the time limits described in the written client-worker service agreement; (4) agreement must be obtained regarding the data to be gathered by the collateral, the way in which this will be presented, and the times when information will be exchanged; (5) the resource person must be willing to work as a member of a team, respecting the fact that the social worker will function as team coordinator; and (6) the collateral must be willing to participate in group conferences when necessary. You can use the checklist in Figure 6.1 to review case management skills used by your staff. Workers can use this to guide their decisions in a case manager role.

Worker _____   Date _____

Item	Client 1	Client 2	Client 3	Client 4
1. Clear objectives have been identified.				
2. Resources selected are most likely to achieve objectives as demonstrated by their prior track record.				
3. A time limit has been set to achieve each objective.				
4. An agreement between the worker and involved resource persons has been written and signed by participants.				
5. Each resource person has agreed to pursue objectives within a set time.				
6. Each resource person has agreed to share data with the worker according to the schedule described in the contract.				
7. Each resource person has agreed to meet with the worker as necessary.				
8. A verbal agreement exists between the worker and the resource persons concerning the above items.				

Figure 6.1 Checklist for Assessing Case Management Skills

PRACTICE TASK 6.3

What criteria do your workers use to decide whether to offer direct services to a client or use a collateral resource?

PRACTICE TASK 6.4

What criteria do your workers use to select collateral resources?

PRACTICE TASK 6.5

What criteria do you use to evaluate how well your workers coordinate services provided to clients?

METHODS USED TO
COORDINATE SERVICES

Methods suggested for coordinating services include use of computers, team approaches, and the use of contracts.

COMPUTERS

Computers can be used to collect data for administrative purposes, for example to tally the number of requests for different services, to track cases and coordinate services, to maintain resource directories and case records, and as an aid in decision making.

Case Tracking

Case tracking is used to monitor the movement of clients from one locality to another and to coordinate services by keeping track of services offered and plans implemented (U.S. Department of Health, Education and Welfare, 1978). Monitoring client movement ensures that families reported to child abuse and neglect registries do not escape investigation by moving out of town. Computers in different locations are linked to a central data base, which a worker can search using descriptors such as a social security number, family name, or child's name. The use of phonetic "sounds-like" searches aids in this process (Cysis-Data Newsletter, 1981). In a sounds-like search, the computer scans its data base for names that are phonetically similar to the name entered into the computer. For example, a search for the Smith family could produce files on families named Smyth and Smythe. Characteristics of the latter families, such as number and ages of children, can be compared to characteristics of the Smith family to determine whether they are the same families.

The Nashville-Davidson project illustrates the use of computers for service coordination and case monitoring (Burt and Balyeat, 1977). This system relies on a computerized data bank in which socioeconomic, diagnostic, and service delivery information on each child receiving services is stored. This system is linked with all service delivery resources. By having each resource supply information on services provided, workers are able to track each child's movement and services received through the entire system. Ideally, duplication of service can be detected and eliminated, and unmet needs can be identified. An agency computer has been linked with the computer system of the juvenile court in a project jointly sponsored by the Institute For Societal Research and the National Council of Juvenile and Family Court Judges (Cysis-Data Newsletter, 1981). This system is used to schedule judicial reviews, to provide information for review and to incorporate judicial orders into individualized case plans.

Use of Computer by
Supervisors and Workers

Computers can be used to store case records and resource directories as well as to facilitate decisions. Standardized forms used for manual recording can be programmed to appear on the computer screen, and workers type case information directly into the computer, eliminating manual recording (Baker et al., 1981; Sullivan, 1982). The use of data-based management systems that generate forms directly on a computer screen and that allow entry of information using a typewriter-like keyboard has reduced many of the problems once associated with computer use, such as precoding of data for entry. The information entered when case records are computerized should be available whether records are kept manually or on an automated system. Retrieval of information is a major advantage of computerized case records. You can monitor worker activity and case progress by searching the records of cases in your unit using descriptors such as worker-client visits and parent-child visits.

A computerized data base of resource information can be an invaluable aid for staff. For example, a worker can ask the computer how many beds are available in nursing homes located within set geographic boundaries or how many placements are available for a fifteen-year-old female adolescent within a certain school district. If a desired placement is located, it can be reserved on the computer, which then alerts other related units — for example, by informing an income maintenance unit to redirect payments to a new setting (Baker et al., 1981).

The capacity of computers to increase reliability in worker decision making is being explored (Bommer et al., 1977; Boyd et al., 1980).

Decision support systems (DSS) require the creation of a data base in which cases are profiled. Each profile includes descriptive case information, such as presenting problem, age, and sex of family members, services provided, activities of service providers and the outcome of activities and services. A DSS developed by Schoech & Schkade (1980) illustrates the use of a computerized DSS. Let's say a worker must decide whether to place a child in out-of-home care. The worker begins by telling the computer that he wants to identify key activities taken in cases similar to the one for which a decision must be made. A series of questions appear on the computer screen. Questions might include the number and ages of children and parents, income and its source, whether either parent has been in prison, and questions related to the family's service history. The computer will inform the worker of the number of cases that are similar to the one described and will note exceptions in similar cases; for example, in the most similar case the age of siblings may differ. The computer will provide a case summary including decisions made, services offered, and outcome. Management information systems now exist for registering child abuse and neglect cases. These systems are programmed to permit tracking of children in placement and to provide aggregate data for supervisors and other administrators, eliminating the need for each agency to develop its own system (Cysis-Data Newsletter, 1982).

Decision support systems are still in a developmental stage. One problem is identification of exemplary cases to serve as reference points against which workers check their decisions. Given the wealth of material that must be managed in order to offer effective services, it is likely that on-line computerized information systems will be increasingly popular. Standardized forms for gathering information will be helpful in resolving problems caused by variations in the quality and quantity of information provided.

TEAM APPROACHES

The use of service delivery teams is growing rapidly (Helfer and Schmidt, 1976; Office of Human Development, 1975). For example, in children's services divisions, teams may include child welfare workers, psychiatrists, psychologists, public health officials, school personnel, attorneys, and juvenile court judges. If team membership remains relatively constant, difficulties such as lack of trust in the capabilities of each team member and concern that confidentiality will not be maintained, should diminish. Designating responsibility for problem solving should be simplified as team members become familiar with

each person's competencies. Regular staff meetings, with all participants present, should eliminate misunderstandings regarding desired
outcomes and the time limits within which these are to be accomplished. Since decision-making responsibilities are diffused across team
members, decisions may be reached more quickly, and there may be a
greater willingness to take risks for which any one person may be
reluctant to accept responsibility.

It is generally agreed that one person must assume the role of team
coordinator or case manager (e.g., Weinrich et al., 1977; Pike et al.,
1977). For example, the child welfare worker, particularly in court
cases in which she is the court representative, is the most likely
candidate for this position. Different models of team management are
available. Common elements assigned to the team manager include the
following: (1) initiating planning activities and keeping track of progress
made; (2) making referrals to other agencies, coordinating the activities
of those agencies, and ensuring that activities are in keeping with the
overall case plans; (3) making decisions — alone, when necessary —
that are most likely to result in effective service provision; and (4) a
willingness to share decision-making responsibilities with other team
members.

CONTRACTS

Written agreements between agencies can be used to coordinate
services. These should clearly describe responsibilities of each participant, criteria for evaluating progress, and expected dates of accomplishment of objectives. The procedures used by Alameda Project staff to
coordinate service delivery were a step in this direction (Stein et al.,
1978). The worker wrote clearly specified objectives based on assessment information, describing what should be different as a result of
participating in a program. In selecting collateral resources, the
worker's first task was to determine whether the resource could achieve
the desired outcomes. This was not difficult, given knowledge about the
intervention procedures used by a collateral as well as knowledge of the
empirical literature describing the results of such procedures in relation
to given problem areas. The case manager must then find out whether
the resource person was willing to work toward the specified objectives
within a time frame that appeared feasible. The resource person had to
agree to share information, in writing, on an agreed-upon schedule. He
also had to agree that if he and the client agreed to work on other
outcomes, these should not take precedence over work on the problem
for which a referral was made. A referral list was made of persons with

This agreement is entered into between _____, child welfare worker, Dr. _____, psychiatrist in private practice, and Ms. _____, public health nurse, each of whom is a service provider in the _____ case. The objective of this agreement is to establish a framework for coordinating services. The outcomes to be attained by each person are described below. A procedure for exchanging information is described and time limits are noted.

1. Ms. _____, public health nurse, agrees to assess the mother's knowledge and skills in selected areas related to infant care. Areas of concern are the client's knowledge of proper nutrition for an infant and skill in menu planning, bathing, diapering, and dressing an infant. In addition, she agrees to assess the mother's ability to discriminate between physical conditions, such as diaper rash, requiring medical attention and those the mother is able to remedy herself. Ms. _____ will conduct this assessment in accordance with her professional training. If problems are identified in any of these areas, Ms. _____ agrees to develop and implement a plan to teach new skills or increase present skills to a level considered acceptable for the infant's safety. She also agrees to gather data regarding progress made in enhancing skill levels.

2. Dr. _____, psychiatrist, agrees to conduct a psychiatric evaluation of Mrs. _____. This will be conducted in whatever manner Dr. _____ deems appropriate. The objective of this evaluation is to address the question of whether Mrs. _____ is able to resume full-time care of her infant son.

3. Ms. _____, child welfare worker, will be responsible for assessment of parent-child interaction in all areas she deems appropriate that are not covered by Ms. _____, public health nurse, or by Dr. _____, psychiatrist. She further agrees to develop, implement, and evaluate appropriate plans for enhancing needed parenting skills, or to contract with another agency to do so. Ms. _____ agrees to gather, summarize, and report to the court all information supplied by Ms. _____ and Dr. _____. If problems arise in terms of achieving objectives, Ms. _____ agrees to call and chair any necessary meetings to try and resolve these.

While it is recognized that work with the mother may extend beyond the assigned tasks, all parties agree (1) not to extend their work into any area specifically assigned to one of the other parties; and (2) to give priority to fulfilling objectives for which they were brought into this case. If problems arise that hinder goal attainment, both Ms. _____ and Dr. _____ agree to attend any necessary meetings. Ms. _____ and Dr. _____ agree to submit final reports to Ms. _____ by _____. This contract is in effect for a period of sixty (60) days: _____ to _____.

Signed: _____, _____
      Ms. _____, Child Welfare Worker   Date

_____, _____
      Ms. _____, Public Health Nurse   Date

_____, _____
      Dr. _____, Psychiatrist   Date

Figure 6.2 Service Coordination Agreement

skills in certain areas as well as a willingness to work within the project's framework. Clients were asked to sign consent forms regarding exchanges of information.

If duplication of services occurred, meetings were arranged and attended by all persons involved in a case. The purpose of such meetings was to clarify any misunderstanding regarding the respective roles of participants and to reaffirm the agreement that participants would not involve themselves in areas other than those for which they were brought into the case. The project worker assumed responsibility for calling and chairing meetings and for gathering and summarizing all information supplied. These procedures resolved a great many difficulties in the use of collateral resources. Written agreements between resources should further clarify expectations (see Figure 6.2).

IMPORTANCE OF UP-TO-DATE INFORMATION ABOUT COLLATERAL RESOURCES

Your workers should have an up-to-date list of available resources, together with specific, up-to-date information concerning resources provided by each source. This information should be readily available via a computerized program, or a card file accessible to all unit staff. One of your important tasks is to make sure that an up-to-date list exists and that this is kept up-to-date. Information noted about an agency should be accompanied by the date this was gathered. Eligibility requirements should be noted, as well as the likelihood that applicants will receive a service or resource. Vague entries such as "gives food" should be avoided. Who is likely to receive this food?

Keeping information about resources up-to-date is easier when each agency assumes responsibility for clearly describing their services and eligibility requirements. Each agency should publish a brochure containing this information and send copies to other agencies. This would involve a cost in terms of writing time, printing, and postage. It would probably entail an even larger cost to agencies in terms of funding sources, clearly seeing, perhaps for the first time, exactly what an agency does and does not provide. In the long run, a great deal of time, money, and energy would be saved by both clients and social workers in pursuing fictional resources. Also, shouldn't funding sources base decisions on an accurate rather than vague, and possibly inaccurate, description of an agency's services?

PRACTICE TASK **6.6**

Find out whether your workers have up-to-date information on resources. If they do not, design a procedure to provide this.

PRACTICE TASK **6.7**

Identify major problems your workers face in coordinating services.

PRACTICE TASK **6.8**

Select the problem mentioned in Practice Task 6.7 that you believe is most amenable to change. Plan, together with your staff, how to resolve this problem.

SUMMARY

Effective service often requires coordination of many resources. Effective coordination requires clear identification of desired outcomes; familiarity with the problem-solving approach employed by resources and their efficiency and effectiveness with given problems; and an agreement by each resource person to work on identified problems within a given time frame, to gather agreed-upon data regarding progress, to share data with the case manager on a predetermined time schedule, and a willingness to work as a member of a team and to participate in group conferences. The use of written agreements between workers and resource persons offers a helpful tool for clarifying expectations and, thus, for facilitating effective service coordination.

Chapter 7

ENCOURAGING EFFECTIVE
STAFF BEHAVIOR

One of your responsibilities is to clearly identify behaviors and goals that will be helpful in offering high-quality services to clients. You must also help staff members determine their own levels of competency in relation to required skills, and help them to enhance these and to gradually assume greater responsibility for maintaining a high level of performance. Staff also have a responsibility for helping to identify skills they should acquire or enhance. You must arrange prompts and incentives that will be helpful in establishing and maintaining effective performance.

You will have to make decisions about what changes to seek and how to achieve these in the most positive and timely way. Some supervisors use exhortation; that is, they verbally encourage workers to act in a different manner and offer reasons that they should. This procedure is notoriously ineffective in changing behavior. One reason for its wide use is the attitude that social workers *should* perform effectively: "They oughta wanna" (Mager and Pipe, 1970: 9).

You could, of course, do nothing; that is, ignore the performance discrepancy and bemoan the fact that things are this way. This often happens following unsuccessful attempts to exhort workers to meet expected standards. You could punish inappropriate behaviors. If a worker consistently refuses to turn in reports on time, a negative statement to this effect could be placed in her personnel folder, and she may receive frequent verbal criticism. Another possibility, however, is to offer positive incentives; for example, a worker could be offered time for special projects for specific levels of performance. In our experience, supervisors find the last possibility the least appealing. They ask, "Why should you offer something to a worker who is not doing her job? She should *want* to do her job." The readiness to use punishment seems to be related to a reluctance to offer positive incentives to a worker for "doing what she should do anyway." A second objection is that offering special incentives to a worker who is doing poorly is not fair to workers who are doing well. This position assumes that workers who are doing well do not receive positive incentives, when in fact, to maintain effective performance, positive incentives should be offered. It also assumes that people always want what others get, and this is not necessarily the case, because people develop their own personal standards against which they evaluate their performance. Workers differ in terms of their skill levels, and it seems only reasonable that incentives be offered on an individual basis. Offering one group member a special incentive for a given outcome usually does not create complaints of unfairness perhaps due to reasons mentioned above, which are shared with the group members (Hayes, 1976; Kazdin, 1977). If this is a problem, then a group contingency could be used in which all group members gain some agreed-upon incentive contingent on an increased level of performance by one or more group members.

The key question is, "What is your goal?" Your goal should not be to withhold extra goodies from a worker who is not performing as expected. Your goal should be to help your workers offer high-quality services to their clients. A focus on agency goals should help you to make decisions about whether changes are required. If a worker is not offering effective services, something should be done. Since exhortation will probably be ineffective, you have a choice between punishing ineffective performance or arranging reminders and offering positive incentives for desired behaviors and outcomes. The latter procedure is most likely to be effective and to generate good feelings between you and your staff as well as increase good feelings by staff about the quality of their work. In addition, offering positive incentives, including praise for specific accomplishments, provides a model for your staff of reinforcers they can offer themselves. This source of positive feedback (self-reinforcement) should help to maintain effective work after temporary incentives offered to increase performance levels are removed. It is important to recognize that the positive incentives offered to encourage more effective behavior are often temporary. As performance improves, the same incentives can be offered for higher performance levels, and, as self-reinforcement assumes more influence over behavior, the levels of reinforcement offered to a worker can approach those offered to all unit staff. The procedures discussed in this chapter for encouraging more effective performance offer an alternative to the oughta-wanna stance. Often, when the consequences following effective behavior are examined, it is not surprising that workers don't wanna.

The following questions will help you identify factors related to performance discrepancies. Is the discrepancy clearly described; that is, can you and involved staff clearly describe and agree on what should be done differently? Have examples of desired behaviors and outcomes been given to staff? Can the worker observe other staff engaging in the desired behavior and being rewarded for doing so? Have incentives been arranged that will support desired behaviors; for example, does it really make any difference in terms of consequences to the worker whether or not he keeps up-to-date logs of his contacts with each client? Have facilitating conditions been arranged that encourage the behavior, such as a form that can be used to record contacts? These questions are explored in more detail in the following sections.

PRACTICE TASK 7.1

List some procedures you use to increase the quality of performance of your staff? Place a plus by those procedures that have been effective and a minus by those that are not as effective as you would like.

IDENTIFYING FACTORS RELATED TO PERFORMANCE DISCREPANCIES

When a needed change is noted, the first importance step is to clearly describe the desired outcome — that is, to describe exactly what the worker should do differently. An example from the area of child welfare might be to keep an up-to-date log of parent-child visits for each case where natural parents are available and the goal is return of children to their biological parents. Such a log may include date, place, duration, purpose, and outcome of visit for each contact. "Up-to-date" may mean that information is to be recorded within one day after each visit. An example of a completed log that illustrates what is required should be available to staff, as well as blank forms to use in their own cases. Research in supervision shows that clear identification of the goals of supervision results in selection of training methods that speed up acquisition of new skills (Lambert, 1980). Vague goals will decrease the likelihood that desired changes will occur. Example of such goals are, "Pay more attention to natural parents"; "Be more interested in work"; and "Be more receptive to supervision."

After clearly describing what should be different, you should then decide whether the performance discrepancy is important (see Figure

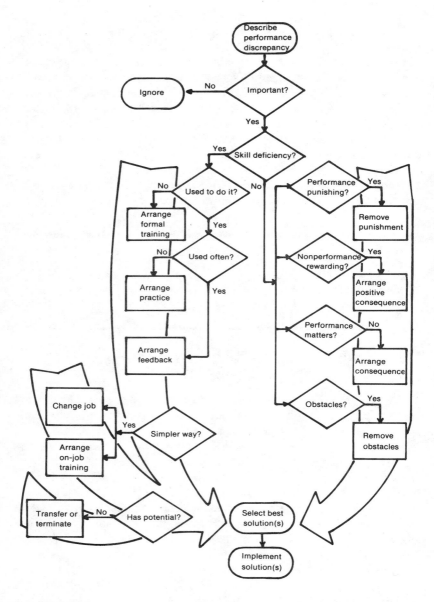

SOURCE: R. F. Mager and P. Pipe, *Analyzing Performance Problems* (p. 92). Copyright © 1970 by Pitman Learning, Inc. Reprinted by permission.

Figure 7.1   Flowchart for Analyzing Performance Problems

7.1). If the answer is no, then it should be ignored (Mager and Pipe, 1970). If it does make a difference, you must then decide whether a skill deficiency is involved, or whether faulty cueing and incentive arrangements are involved. Supervisors often try to find out if a worker has required skills by simply asking, "Do you know how to do _____ ?" or by asking for a verbal description of the skill. For example, if you are trying to find out if a worker knows how to specify clear objectives, you may ask her how this can be accomplished, and the worker may be able to give a verbal description as well as examples of specified objectives. The ability to do this does not necessarily mean that she can specify clear objectives in her own cases. The best way to find out if she has required skills to accomplish this is to observe her trying to do so.

PRACTICE TASK 7.2

What procedures do you use to identify factors related to performance discrepancies of your staff?

PRACTICE TASK 7.3

Give three examples of performance discrepancies on the part of your staff that you decided were not really worth bothering with.

PRACTICE TASK 7.4

Give two examples of behaviors on the part of higher-level administration that you decided were not really worth bothering with.

If a worker does have the skills required to perform a task — such as keeping a log of contacts with clients — but does not do so, four possible reasons should be explored (Mager and Pipe, 1970).

Expected behaviors may be punished. Expected performance may result in negative consequences. Let us say that a worker tries to (1) increase visits between biological parents and their children who are in foster care and (2) observe parent-child interaction during visits. Negative consequences that may result include an increase in workload and criticism from foster parents for arranging visits with a mother who is a "bad influence." People avoid doing things that result in unpleasant

outcomes. Questions related to the possibility of punishing consequences include the following (Mager and Pipe, 1970: 59):

— What consequences result from acting as expected?

— Is it punishing to act as expected?

— Does the person perceive performance as resulting in penalties?

— Would her world become a little dimmer (to her) if she acted as
  expected?

Nonperformance may be rewarding. It is important to "determine
whether nonperformance or other performance leads to more favorable
consequences than desired performance" (Mager and Pipe, 1970: 69).
Perhaps you offer extra attention to workers who do not carry out
expected tasks. Not taking time to try to locate required resources
leaves more time for other tasks in a busy work schedule. Useful
questions to pose include the following (p. 69):

— What is the result of doing it his way instead of my way?

— What does he get out of his present performance in the way of
  rewards, prestige, and status?

— Does he get more attention for inappropriate than for appropriate behavior?

It may not be reinforcing to act in expected ways. Neither you nor
fellow workers may provide any positive feedback for attempting to
locate needed resources. Here the important determination that must be
made is "whether there is a meaningful consequence for the desired
performance" (p. 77). Questions to ask include the following (p. 77):

— Does performing as desired really matter to the person?

— Are there any favorable outcomes for expected behaviors?

— Are there undesirable outcomes for not offering expected
  behaviors?

As Mager and Pipe (p. 67) point out, "Often, people cling to the old
because there is no real reason, no favorable consequence to them, for
doing it the new way. It is more comfortable, more pleasant, more
rewarding to stay with the old."

PRACTICE TASK **7.5**

List three behaviors you would like to see more often and identify what consequences you now offer for these behaviors. (Note who is involved.)

What I would like to
see more often: Consequences I now offer:

PRACTICE TASK **7.6**

List three behaviors you would like to see less often and note what you do following these behaviors. (Identify who is involved.)

What I would like to
see less often: Consequences I now offer:

There may be obstacles to acting in expected ways. Workers may dislike confronting biological parents with the need to work toward a permanent living arrangement for their child. Time may be limited because of heavy caseloads. Perhaps you have not made your expectations clear. If desired outcomes and competencies are not clearly described, it is difficult if not impossible to identify how to rearrange prompts and incentives to increase these outcomes. The statement "use more effective case management procedures" is vague.

One component of a systematic case management procedure is keeping a log of all contacts with clients (and attempts to contact clients if this is also important). Workers typically include this information in narratives; thus it must be laboriously culled from lengthy case records. Simply asking workers to keep such a log will probably not be sufficient to encourage them to do it. A form should be provided that facilitates recording. Where the form is to be kept and what information is to be recorded should be clearly described, as well as when information should be recorded. Incentives should be arranged that reward workers who keep logs according to agreed-upon expectations.

Questions that are helpful in identifying obstacles include the following:

— What prevents expected behavior?
— Does he know what is expected?
— Does he know when to do what is expected?
— Are there conflicting demands on his time?

— Does he lack authority? the time? the tools?

— Is he restricted by policies or by a "right way of doing it" "how we've always done it" that ought to be changed?

— Can I reduce visual and auditory distractions?

— Can I reduce distracting phone calls and the demands of less importance problems?

— Are necessary tools, such as forms, readily available?

These reasons suggest the following questions. Does anything positive happen following desired behavior, and, if so, how important are such consequences? Is any unpleasant event removed following the behavior? Does anything unpleasant follow the behavior, and, if so, how unpleasant are these events? Are other behaviors more reinforcing? Are required skills available?

What happens before behaviors of concern is also important. Have cues been arranged to remind workers to carry out behaviors? Are necessary tools such as forms readily available? Are contexts available that will facilitate desired behaviors, such as periods of quiet in which to write reports? (See Figure 7.2.)

You may find it helpful to diagram the consequences related to a desired outcome. Let us take the example of clarity of handwriting, which is a topic of concern to many supervisors, let alone to workers and clerks who must try to read the handwritten reports. We will define clear handwriting as writing that 90 percent of your staff can read with ease. Probable consequences for unclear handwriting are that the worker

(1)   is able to complete reports faster;

(2)   has more time for other tasks;

(3)   receives no reaction from supervisors, fellow workers, or clerks.

Probable consequences for clear handwriting are that the worker

(1)   takes more time;

(2)   receives no reaction from supervisors, fellow workers, or clerks;

(3)   has less time for other tasks.

Desired Behavior: _____

Description of how behavior will be counted: _____

Antecedents			Consequences		
Skills Needed			**Positive consequences that follow desired behavior**		
Available	Not available	Should be arranged		Now available	Should be arranged
Cues that remind worker			**Negative consequences that are removed following desired behavior**		
	Available	Should be arranged		Now removed	Should be rearranged
Tools that facilitate behavior			**Unpleasant consequences that follow desired behavior**		
	Available	Should be arranged		Now present	Should be removed
Contexts that facilitate behavior			**Related undesirable behaviors that are reinforced**		
	Available	Should be arranged		Now reinforced	Plan for rearrangement

SOURCE: Gambrill and Stein (1978: 200).

Figure 7.2 Factors Related to a Desired Performance

Antecedents related to unclear handwriting may be any of the following:

(1) Worker does not know how to write clearly (skill deficit).
(2) No cues are available to remind the worker to write clearly.
(3) Forms often contain inadequate space for material (inadequate tools).
(4) Offices are noisy and interruptions frequent (nonfacilitating context).

If this picture of the current situation is correct, it is not surprising that there is so much unclear handwriting. Typically, no unpleasant consequences befall people who write poorly, although there may be many unexpressed nasty thoughts about their handwriting and even about the people themselves. Also, there are no positive consequences for workers who do have clear handwriting. Antecedents that may encourage clear handwriting — such as a note reminding workers to write clearly — typically are not provided.

If the quality of your workers' performance does not match your expectations, you should explore antecedents and consequences related to desired behaviors. You will often discover that no positive consequences follow the behavior. In addition, negative consequences may follow desired behaviors. Let us say that you ask staff to have a certain report on your desk at a given time and that only 50% of workers meet this deadline. Ask yourself the following questions. Do you provide any positive incentives for turning in reports on time? Do you provide any unpleasant consequences for late reports? Are alternative behaviors more rewarding? Are there obstacles to satisfying your request; if so, what are these and how can they be removed?

PRACTICE TASK 7.7

Identify two behaviors you would like your workers to engage in more frequently. Then identify obstacles that may interfere with these behaviors.

What I would like to
see more often: Obstacles:

DECIDING HOW TO INCREASE
DESIRED BEHAVIOR

Information recorded in Figure 7.2 will be helpful in deciding how to increase desired behaviors. If you find that no positive consequences follow the behaviors you would like to see more often, you should arrange such consequences. If unfavorable outcomes follow these behaviors, you should remove or minimize these. Positive incentives for nonperformance must be removed and required tools, reminders, and contexts provided. You should clearly describe desired outcomes.

REARRANGING POSITIVE OUTCOMES

Meaningful incentives will have to be provided to establish and maintain desired behavior. Public posting of performance has been found to increase desired behavior in some settings (Panyan et al., 1970). A memo instructing staff to lead daily recreational activities for clients in a residential setting for the retarded was compared with two other procedures to determine their relative effectiveness in increasing the frequency of staff-led activities (Quilitch, 1975). The two other procedures consisted of (1) a workshop teaching staff how to lead recreational activities and (2) assigning staff activity leaders and providing performance feedback to staff by publicly posting the daily average number of active residents on each ward. Only the latter procedure was effective in increasing the number of staff-led activities. Verbal and written statements of praise and appreciation offer another source of positive feedback.

Let us assume that unclear handwriting of workers is a major problem for secretaries, supervisors, and fellow workers, and that we are not dealing with a skill deficit — that the individuals involved could write more clearly if they took the time to do so. Incentives for clear handwriting will have to be arranged. Positive incentives may include statements of praise from the supervisor for improvements in clarity of handwriting, as well as such statements from secretaries and fellow workers who read reports from the workers. For example, a secretary might say, "It was so much easier to type your material because your handwriting was clear." In addition to offering positive incentives for desired behavior (clear handwritten material), positive incentives should no longer be presented following inappropriate behavior (hand-writing that is difficult to read). You could return reports to staff that you cannot read together with a request to rewrite the report more clearly. You could instruct secretaries to return handwritten material to staff when they have difficulty reading reports. Additional positive incentives could be provided, such as a public posting of the name of the worker whose clarity of writing improved the most over the past month. Only if different consequences follow clear and unclear handwriting will the probabilities of occurrence of these two types of writing differ. A recent study showed that increased verbal approval of staff performance by supervisors resulted in dramatic increases in appropriate staff behavior (Montegar et al., 1977; see also Quilitch, 1978).

Organizations have explored the effectiveness of a variety of incentives in increasing desired behaviors. The opportunity to play poker was used in a large manufacturing center to decrease absenteeism (Pedalino and Gamboa, 1974). On each day that an employee came to work on time, he could select a card from a deck of playing cards. At the end of a five-day work period, the employee who had the winning poker hand in each department (average size was 25 employees) would win $20. Offering small amounts of money contingent on desired behavior resulted in dramatic increases in such behavior (Patterson et al., 1976).

Many incentives, such as amount of pay, vacation time, training leaves, promotions, and merit increases, are not contingent on the quality of service. It is the rare social service organization that makes even part of an employee's pay contingent on achievement. In one example of such an organization (the Huntsville-Madison County Mental Health Center), increases in salary were linked to counselor performance (Rinn and Vernon, 1975; Bolin and Kivens, 1974). Individual goals were established for each counselor and criteria for evaluation selected for each (Turner and Lee, 1976a, 1976b; Turner and Goodson, 1977). Ratings were made in relation to the performance of the counselor during the prior year or, if the counselor was new, were based on the last person's performance. Extra points could be gained by contracting for changing specific behaviors or by performing extra work, such as gaining additional education to improve on-the-job skills.

> Once the job tasks and criteria are specified and agreed to, they are signed off by the assistant director for administration to ensure consistency of goals across service components. The agreement then becomes a contract between the employee and the center's board of directors [Bolin and Kivens, 1974: 30].

Performance data were collected regularly by the supervisor. These data were available to the employee at all times and were reviewed by the supervisor and supervisee at least quarterly. Random checks were carried out by the assistant director to assess the validity and reliability of data collected. A point system was used to assess each counselor's performance each year. Part of this was based on performance of the five to fifteen tasks for which each counselor individually contracted. A 10 percent raise was awarded for performance in the 95-100 percent range; 8 percent if performance was in the 70-94 percent; 5 percent if it was in the 50-69 percent range; and if performance fell below 49 percent, probation, demotion, or termination followed. A point system was also employed by the center to determine the degree of success achieved with each client.

Lottery systems have been found to be effective in improving staff performance (although such a system may be illegal in certain counties). A performance-based lottery was used to improve the care offered by staff at a residential center for the multiply handicapped retarded (Iwata et al., 1976). Weekly criteria were identified for appropriate staff behavior; for example, being observed changing at least one resident's clothing during daily checks. At the end of the week, slips of paper containing the names of staff who met these criteria were placed in a container. The winner's name was drawn from this container, and this person received the opportunity to rearrange days off from work the next week. Several positive changes resulted from the lottery, including increased staff time spent with residents and better unit supervision. The authors noted, however, that individual performance varied considerably, with only one-third of the staff being eligible to participate in the lottery in a given week.

Providing staff with quantitative information on improvement of assigned patients has been associated with an improvement in patient behavior (Pomerleau et al., 1973). It should be noted, however, that improvement in client behavior may not in itself function as a positive incentive for staff, even when specific feedback is provided concerning progress (Loeber, 1971). This highlights the need the identify other incentives to establish and maintain desired performance levels. The reactions of superiors and fellow workers may serve as a more powerful reinforcer than the behavior of clients (Panyan et al., 1970). Public recognition for accomplishments could be offered during social gatherings such as dinner parties — perhaps a "worker of the month" award and a yearly award. Attention of the media to such events would help to offer a more balanced view of the achievements of social workers; usually only the mistakes of social workers receive press notices.

An agency newsletter would provide many opportunities to offer recognition to line staff, supervisors, and administrators, as well as to acquaint personnel with each other and to acquaint them with training opportunities, and new information (Patterson et al., 1972). New methods that workers have successfully used could be described, and workers could pass on recommendations to supervisors. A quiz (with answers on another page) concerning new information related to agency goals could be include periodically. Expected progress reports at staff meetings offer opportunities to provide positive feedback to staff for their successes. In many agencies, performance reviews are infrequent and, thus, do not support the many small steps involved in effective case management.

Group contingencies offer another way to encourage effective staff performance. For example, some positive incentive, such as a certificate of recognition, could be given to the unit whose members have been most successful in identifying clear objectives in their cases. A training opportunity could be offered to a unit whose members are keeping track of progress made in the highest percentage of their cases. In this type of group contingency, the reinforcer received by group members is contingent on the output of the entire unit. Another type of group contingency, in which a reinforcer offered to group members is contingent on the performance of one person, has been used in classroom settings to improve the performance of one group member (Hayes, 1976). In yet another variation, the incentive offered to group members is available contingent on the performance of a subset of group members; for example, workers who are having difficulty specifying clear objectives. Here, a desired training opportunity could be offered contingent on a 20 percent increase in the number of specified objectives written by staff members in this subset. Such an arrangement has been found to increase peer tutoring efforts (Hayes, 1976).

Feedback concerning progress achieved in meeting client objectives should offer one of the most important sources of reinforcers for staff. This source is often forgone by failure to clearly identify objectives sought and to keep track of progress made. This lack of attention to monitoring progress is probably one of the main reasons for so-called worker burn-out. Without this feedback, a worker cannot know the extent to which plans are succeeding, nor of course, can clients or supervisors.

Discovering reinforcers. One helpful way to discover reinforcers is to watch what people do. For example, do your workers spend time in a staff lounge? Do they enjoy being out of the office? Do they like to attend training meetings? Reinforcers should meet certain important criteria. They must be possible and ethical to offer, they should be nonsatiating (that is, people do not tire of them quickly), and they should be contingent on desired behaviors. Another way to locate reinforcers is to ask people what they would like. You should try to be creative in locating possible incentives.

In addition to access to enjoyable activities (e.g., attending training programs) and verbal statements of praise, another possible source of incentives is freedom from disliked tasks, such as freedom from cleaning the coffee pot, contingent on a certain level of behavior. Feedback about the correctness of decisions made also functions as a reinforcer. Such feedback may be individual or may entail public posting of performance levels or special notices in newsletters or newspapers. Many agencies have no newsletter, thus forgoing a valuable source through which to offer support for accomplishments.

Items identified by observing workers and asking for their preferences could be listed, and staff members could be asked to check the most appealing items. This would generate a list of incentives that could be used. Some examples of reinforcers are listed below.

Time off	Use of agency car
An extra vacation day	Being excused from a meeting
Special project time	Recognition in newspaper or agency newsletter
Greater input in administrative decisions	Selecting a client to add to caseload
Posting of individual performance levels	Posting of group performance levels
Choose office and/or furniture	Time in staff lounge
Select extra assignments	Praise from fellow workers
Recommendation for a promotion	Public praise by supervisors and administrators
Organized activities, such as games and parties	Attend training program
Prizes	Opportunity to talk with supervisor
Preference for holiday and vacation days	Access to a consultant

Recommendation for a pay raise	Praise from clients
Praise from staff in other agencies	Accomplishment of a specific case objective
Increased opportunity for designing and directing program	Less supervision
Longer lunch hour	More secretarial help

The efficiency of clerical staff is closely related to morale in social service agencies. If clerical staff are not meeting expected standards of performance, you should clearly describe the exact nature of these performance discrepancies and explore the contingencies related to these. Do clerical staff receive positive feedback for meeting expected standards? How often? Is this sufficient?

PRACTICE TASK 7.8

Identify ten incentives you could use to increase desired staff behavior. Keep in mind that items selected must be possible and ethical to use, must be made contingent on desired outcomes, and should be nonsatiating; that is, people will not tire of them quickly.

Removing reinforcement for inappropriate behavior. Achieving an increase in effective staff performance will probably require withholding reinforcement following inappropriate behavior, as well as offering positive incentives for appropriate work behavior. For example, secretaries could be instructed to return handwritten reports that are very difficult to read. The squeaky wheel gets grease; thus the worker who complains may receive the most supervisory attention. Complaints may be maintained by decreasing supervisory attention, since they are aversive to the supervisor. If you do not wish to encourage complaints, then you must remove reinforcing consequences for these and must reinforce alternative behaviors — for example, positive statements by the worker. No longer obtaining reinforcement for behaviors that have been rewarded in the past can be unpleasant. One way to avoid this unpleasant reaction is to first increase positive feedback for appropriate behavior so that the overall amount of positive feedback increases rather than decreases.

Removing negative consequences for desired behaviors. It is surprising how often unpleasant consequences follow staff behaviors that you would like to see more frequently. These should be removed or minimized. Provision of more effective services often requires more efficient use of time and energy. The new case review laws in child welfare, for example, will require more time and effort on the part of workers unless arrangements are made to ensure that compliance with these facilitates required tasks. Provision of necessary tools and facilitating contexts should decrease negative consequences of desired behaviors, as discussed below.

Providing necessary tools. You can increase the probability of desired behavior by making sure that necessary or facilitating tools are available. Easy-to-use and readily available forms will make it more probable that these will be completed. Clear guidelines concerning where forms are to be placed in case records will make these easier to find. If a worker types well and is more likely to complete reports if she has access to a typewriter, such access should be arranged, if possible. Answers to the question, "What is necessary to increase the probability of this behavior?" will offer helpful information about required tools.

Rearranging cues. Desired behaviors can also be increased by providing cues that remind staff to offer these. Checklists such as those illustrated in this book can serve this purpose. Humorous posters have been used to improve the quality of services offered by staff (Fielding et al., 1971). Clear expectations and frequent feedback based upon *specific* accomplishments will be very helpful in increasing desired behaviors (e.g., Lambert, 1980; Lovett et al., 1983).

Providing facilitating contexts. The context in which behavior occurs influences its likelihood. A frequent complaint by workers is the difficulty of systematic planning or report writing because of frequent telephone calls and other interruptions. Perhaps a daily "time out" from telephone calls could be arranged, allowing workers a distraction-free time for case planning and report writing; alternatively, a special recording-room could be set aside (Domash et al., 1980).

PRACTICE TASK **7.9**

Identify a change you would like to make in a worker's performance. Select one that is important and be sure to clearly describe the desired behavior. Using the form in Figure 7.2, describe the behavior and the means of evaluating progress. Next, identify current antecedents and consequences related to the change you would like to see and fill in the spaces provided in Figure 7.2. Is it surprising that the desired behavior does not occur more frequently?

Describe how you could rearrange antecedents and consequences to encourage desired outcomes. What positive incentives could you offer? Could you remove negative consequences that follow desired behavior? What tools could you introduce to encourage desired outcomes? Is the performance deficit related to skill deficiencies? If so, you will have to address these first (see Chapter 8).

If you are really serious about making use of the information you have gathered and would like to carry out your plan to see whether it will be effective, the following steps will assist you. First, gather a baseline of the behavior in question; that is, arrange a feasible, relevant way to monitor the behavior or outcome for a week or two to check your assumptions about how often this outcome or behavior occurs. (See Chapter 4 for a description of methods you can use.) You may be able to gather baseline data easily by examination of case records; for example, see how many cases include an up-to-date log of client-worker contacts. Next, implement your plan while continuing to monitor how often the desired outcome occurs. Have you been successful? If not, explore possible reasons for lack of success. If you have been successful, plan how you can remove any artificial components of your program and still maintain desired levels of performance (see Chapter 10).

WORKER-SUPERVISOR AGREEMENTS

You should offer individual feedback to all of your supervisees concerning their strengths and areas in which performance could be improved. A written agreement (Figure 7.3) between you and each of your workers will be helpful in clarifying expectations (Kurtz, 1976; Goldhammer, 1969; Turner and Lee, 1976.) Specific outcomes to pursue should be jointly agreed-upon. Weekly or monthly feedback could be offered in relation to each desired outcome. Changes desired by your supervisees should be included in such agreements (with your permission). Examples of supervisory behaviors that might be of interest to staff are given below.

Increase	Decrease
praise for specific worker behaviors	complaints about vaguely identified worker behaviors
smiles	frowns
loaning copies of helpful articles to workers	making negative comments about workers in the presence of other people
helping out workers in busy times (e.g. taking phone calls)	reading magazines at desk
Clearly describing desired changes in worker behavior	making indirect, unassertive requests for changes in behavior

As when working with clients, it is important to obtain baseline levels of performance when seeking a change in worker behavior. It is always important to start where the person is in terms of current performance levels, so that initial requirements can be achieved. Once high levels of performance are attained, incentives can be offered for maintaining these.

PRACTICE TASK 7.10

Identify a specific worker behavior that you would like to alter, and write a tentative supervisor-worker agreement.

ENCOURAGING AND MAINTAINING SELF-REINFORCING SKILLS

Effective self-reinforcement skills are important in maintaining practice skills. Self-reinforcement involves offering self-statements of praise or external incentives, such as special treats, for achievements. The same characteristics that are important in offering feedback to others are also important when offering self-reinforcement (see Chapter 9). These include being specific, selecting effective reinforcers, and offering these contingent on accomplishments. Self-reinforcement skills may be deficient in a variety of ways. Workers may rarely offer self-praise for accomplishments. Or they may do so, but in an ineffective

This agreement is entered into between _____ ,
social worker, and _____ , supervisor, for the period
_____ through _____ , at which time progress will be reviewed by both _____ and _____ .
The worker agrees to

(1) increase cases in which a counselor-client agreement has been written from
     0 to 25 percent;
(2) increase from 75 to 100% identified goals on all cases in care over two
     weeks.

The supervisor agrees to

(1) review agreements written and offer constructive feedback about their
     adequacy;
(2) allot to _____one-half hour for each acceptable counselor-
     client agreement that is written to work on a special project of
     _____'s choice.

Signed:

_____   _____
Worker   Supervisor

_____
Date

Figure 7.3 Example of a Supervisor-Worker Agreement

manner — for example, offering global statements about themselves,
which they do not believe and which do not offer feedback in relation to
specific accomplishments. They may dilute self-statements of praise
with punishing or belittling statements, such as, "I could have done
better," "I'll never learn how to do this." Questions that will be helpful
in exploring the effectiveness of self-reinforcement skills include the
following:

— Does the worker have an effective repertoire of self-praise
   statements?

— Does she reinforce herself for accomplishment of specific
   goals?

— Does she offer these only if she accomplishes specific tasks?

— Does she dilute self-praise by including negative statements
   about herself or her performance?

Examples of positive self-statements include

- — "Good for me. I completed all recording on time for a week."
- — "I telephoned that lady even though I did not feel like it."
- — "I reminded my secretary that I needed that report this afternoon even though I did not want to."
- — "I clearly defined objectives on three of my cases."

A worker might make an agreement with herself that if she completes her recording on time for the week, she will buy a magazine she has wanted to read. Criteria must be clearly described, allowing her to easily determine whether or not she achieves her goal, and a way of assessing progress must be arranged. You should provide a model for self-evaluation by praising workers for effective behavior in the presence of other staff and by supporting appropriate approval statements on the part of staff concerning their own behavior. (See Practice Task 10.11 in Chapter 10.)

PRACTICE TASK. 7.11

Collect three examples of self-praise from each of your workers. Examine these to see whether they meet the criteria for effective use of positive self-statements. (Use the format shown in Practice Task 10.11).

SUMMARY

It must "make a difference" to people to engage in expected behaviors. Exhortation typically will not result in changes in behavior. Punishment is less effective than use of positive incentives, and it generates bad feelings. Reluctance to use positive incentives because "it is the worker's job to perform effectively" must be reexamined in view of the overriding aim of offering effective service to clients. Rich schedules of positive incentives may be required at first to achieve new performance levels; however, as performance stabilizes, these can be partially removed. You will have to be creative in locating positive incentives that can be used and forming individual agreements with workers in relation to desired changes. Formal training will be required only if skill deficits exist. You should provide models of effective performance.

Chapter 8

GUIDELINES FOR ARRANGING
TRAINING PROGRAMS

Use of a systematic decision-making procedure will require new skills on the part of staff, such as skill in identifing clear objectives. You are the most reasonable person to fill some training needs because you have close contact with unit staff. "Supervision is an administrative process with an educational purpose" (Towle, 1954: 132). It is clear from Kadushin's survey of supervisors that the educational component of supervision is a valued aspect of that role (Kadushin, 1976). This chapter offers guidelines that will help you to select training programs for your staff. You will have to decide what criteria to use to choose programs. Questions of concern include the following: Who will benefit from this training program? Is there any evidence that this program will result in better services for clients?

A great deal is known about the optimal conditions for learning new skills. Many of these points are so obvious that they are easy to lose sight of.

IS THE PROBLEM A
SKILL DEFICIENCY?

In Chapter 7 we noted the importance of carefully describing desired outcomes as a first step in improving performance — to clearly define what the worker should do differently. The question should then be asked, "Does the desired behavior really matter?" If the answer is yes, the next step is to determine whether the performance discrepancy is caused by a skill deficit. One way to determine whether a skill deficit is involved is to ask: If his life depended on it, would he still not do it (Mager and Pipe, 1970: 17)? Let's say that the answer is no. As Mager and Pipe point out, if the worker successfully carried out the behavior in the past but is presently not doing so, then lack of feedback is the probable culprit. If the worker used the skill in the past but now rarely does so, then a lack of practice may be the cause (see Figure 7.1). Skills can erode when there is a lack of feedback concerning their effectiveness. The need for feedback on an ongoing basis for the maintenance of effective behaviors was stressed in Chapter 7. Skills can also erode from lack of practice.

PRACTICE TASK **8.1**

What procedures do you use to distinguish between a skill deficit and a motivational problem (i.e., more rewarding incentives must be offered)?

IS FORMAL TRAINING NEEDED?

The next step is to explore the possibility that a simple solution exists, other than formal training (Mager and Pipe, 1970). For example, checklists can be used to remind workers of the steps involved in a procedure (see Chapter 3 for examples). Computer terminals can be used to review outcome categories of cases. Performance aids could be used, such as files, color-coded in terms of outcome category and length of time in care. Perhaps needed skills can be learned through informal observation of effective models and on-the-job training. This step of exploring the feasibility of simple solutions to performance deficits is often overlooked.

PRACTICE TASK **8.2**

Give three examples of simple procedures that you use to remind workers about important tasks.

COMPONENTS OF EFFECTIVE
TRAINING PROGRAMS

Ingredients of effective training programs include (1) clear identification of objectives; (2) identification of component skills required to attain objectives; (3) description of current skill levels in relation to objectives; (4) identification of a way to monitor progress; (5) development of an effective training program and provision for alteration of the program as needed; (6) arrangement for on-the-job practice of new skills; and (7) arrangement for ongoing feedback (see Figure 8.1).

_____ 1. Outcomes to be achieved through use of new skills are clearly described.
_____ 2. Skills required to achieve these outcomes are clearly described.
_____ 3. Intermediate skills are described.
_____ 4. Clear criteria are identified for assessing whether each skill is present, and for monitoring progress.
_____ 5. Each trainee's initial repertoire is evaluated in the situation in which the skill will be used.
_____ 6. Objectives are directly related to required on-the-job tasks.
_____ 7. A step-by-step learning format is used.
_____ 8. More advanced material is withheld until mastery of earlier steps is achieved.
_____ 9. Models of effective performance are presented.
_____ 10. Models of inappropriate behavior are presented.
_____ 11. Desirable behaviors are clearly identified during model presentation.
_____ 12. Trainee attention to modeled behavior is arranged.
_____ 13. Practice opportunities are offered.
_____ 14. Immediate feedback on performance is offered based on previously identified criteria and on each trainee's initial skill levels.
_____ 15. Constructive feedback is provided in which progress related to specific behaviors is first noted (see Chapter 9).
_____ 16. Opportunities for model presentation, practice, and feedback are offered as necessary.
_____ 17. Arrangements are made for trainees to gradually assume responsibility for evaluating their behavior based on specific criteria.
_____ 18. Trainees have opportunities to train others in skills they have learned.
_____ 19. A monitoring system has been designed and implemented so that outcomes achieved through use of new skills can be tracked on the job.
_____ 20. Individual worker-supervisor agreements are made for specific performance changes.

SOURCE: Gambrill and Stein (1978: 209).

Figure 8.1 Checklist for Evaluating Training Programs

PRACTICE TASK 8.3

List the criteria you use to judge the quality of training programs offered to your staff.

IDENTIFYING OBJECTIVES AND COMPONENT SKILLS

The first requisite of a training program is deciding what skills the trainee should acquire as a result of the program and under what circumstances these skills should occur. Progress has been uneven in identifying competencies involved in offering effective services. Considerable progress has been made in describing different levels of empathy, and programs have been designed to teach this skill (e.g., Ivy and

Authier, 1978). Progress has not been striking in determining the relationship between levels of empathy offered and outcomes achieved (Lambert et al., 1978). We have not had much success in identifying the skills involved in conducting a successful assessment interview or in selecting the best procedure or procedural mix for a given presenting problem. However, efforts within competency-based education in interpersonal helping are encouraging (see for example, Clark et al., 1979; Gambrill, 1983). Competency-based education is characterized by an attempt to identify areas of competence and specific skills in each area, by design of a method to assess whether skills are present, by development of effective training programs, and by ongoing evaluation of performance. In a competency-based education program developed by Brockway et al. (1977), trainees must demonstrate skills in four areas before they receive letters of recommendation from their supervisors: (1) clinical interviewing and communication; (2) empirically based assessment and treatment; (3) knowledge of human growth and development; and (4) the ability to think analytically.

DESCRIPTION OF CURRENT SKILLS

Clear description of objectives and component behaviors will facilitate identification of a current skill level, because it will indicate what to look for. Let's say that you would like to help your staff learn to identify clear objectives. You should first review case records to determine how objectives are currently defined. You should also evaluate staff's skills in this area during role plays in which examples are offered and workers are asked to provide clear objectives. You should make these role plays as life-like as possible. Assessment during role plays serves two functions: (1) to discover a person's ability to construct competencies, that is, to find out what a person can do in a specific situation; and (2) to find out what that person usually does. (Information about what a person usually does in a situation may not indicate what they could do.) The data you gather may indicate that objectives identified by your staff do not meet the requisites of a specified objective in one or more ways. (A specified objective indicates what is to be done by whom, where and when, and with what frequency, duration, or other relevant measure, such as latency. (Intermediate steps should also be described.) Criteria for determining whether an objective has been achieved should be clear. Description of initial skill levels will allow you to use a constructive approach to training, in which programs build on available assets. This also allows feedback concerning progress.

Observation of behavior in real-life contexts offers the best source of information about what workers actually do when with clients, significant others, and other professionals. Process records, for example, do not accurately represent what takes place during social workers' meetings with clients (Kadushin, 1976). A comparison of observers' ratings of videotaped clinical interviews conducted by medical students in their psychiatric clerkship and students' self-reports of these interviews revealed that 54% of the themes identified by observers were not reported by the students in their supervisory sessions (Muslin et al., 1981). If you would like to assess a worker's interviewing skills, you should observe some of their interviews with clients. Clients usually readily agree to such observation if the reasons for this are explained and confidentiality assured. If a worker asks you to help him improve his parent training skills, you could accompany him to a client's home and watch what he does or observe his behavior in role plays. Observation in role plays or real-life contexts offers more accurate material than do verbal reports and should result in more helpful feedback to workers. Honoring the norm of constructive feedback will make this an educational, supportive experience rather than a threatening one (see Chapter 9).

PRACTICE TASK 8.4

Indicate how often you use each of the following methods to examine competency levels of your staff using a scale ranging from 1 (not at all) to 5 (very often).

1 2 3 4 5

(1) Supervisee's written records
(2) Supervisee's verbal reports
(3) Audiotapes of worker-client interaction
(4) Videotapes of worker-client interaction
(5) Observation of worker-client interaction through one-way mirror
(6) Observation of worker-client office interviews
(7) Observation of worker in real-life settings
(8) Observation of worker's activity during group supervisory sessions
(9) Observation of worker's activity in staff meetings
(10) Client evaluations of worker performance
(11) Worker's statistical forms

(12) Quantitative measures of progress achieved in attaining client desired outcomes
(13) Other (please describe)

PRACTICE TASK **8.5**

Do you tend to use direct (observation of behavior) or indirect methods (e.g., self-report) to identify competencies of your staff? (Review your answers to Task 8.4.)

Be sure to focus on the outcomes to be achieved through use of skills. If you lose sight of these, you may increase skills that have little relevance for helping clients achieve desired outcomes. If no information is available concerning skills required to achieve a certain outcome, you will have to carry out a task analysis, in which component skills are identified (see, for example, Gael, 1983; Pettes, 1979; Mager, 1962; Sheafer and Jenkins, 1982).

THE DESIGN OF EFFECTIVE TRAINING PROGRAMS

A great deal is known about the ingredients of effective training programs (Gagne, 1977; also see Figure 8.1). One of the most important components is arrangement for sequential learning in which easy skills are first established, allowing positive feedback. Only after easier skills are mastered should additional requirements be made. Access to more advanced material should not be permitted until the trainee has demonstrated competency in earlier units.

Training programs often fail to provide examples of both effective and ineffective models of desired competencies; nor do they ensure that workers pay attention to models presented, in which case trainees may become bored. Other inadequacies include failure to arrange for practice of new behavior in settings that are similar or identical to those in which skills will be used, lack of immediate constructive feedback, and failure to use sequential learning. The importance of actually using skills is supported by many studies (e.g., Martin, 1972). Models may be presented in a variety of ways, including audiotape, videotape, film, or written examples (e.g., Gray, 1974). For example, the steps involved in defining clear objectives could be described in writing and modeled during staff meetings. Peer tutors could be involved in training programs for economical as well as educational purposes; usually, both the tutor and the peer gain educational benefits. Trainees could work in pairs, each becoming familiar not only with her own projects but also with those of her partner.

Process rather than outcome measures are often used to evaluate the effectiveness of training programs. Let us say for example that workers attend a training program in family therapy. Process measures of the quality of the program might include whether workers acquire certain skills, such as identification of rules used within a family and assessment of interaction patterns among family members. These skills may or may not be related to being more (or less) successful in achieving specific agreed-upon outcomes with families. A focus only on process outcomes often deflects attention from the possibility that these may not actually produce more effective services to clients. Training programs are often evaluated in terms of how much trainees liked the program. Here, too, there may or may not be a relationship between the measure used (liking a program) and offering more effective services.

In evaluating training programs, it may be helpful to use a checklist noting important components of such programs (see Figure 8.1). This will indicate how programs could be improved. Incentives could be offered by workers and administrators to supervisors for improving the percentage of effective components included in the training programs they arrange.

Recognition of individual differences in available competencies and styles calls for a greater use of individual contracts in relation to behaviors to be changed (Kurtz, 1976; Hart, 1982; Goldhammer, 1969; Munson, 1981; also see example in Chapter 7). Workers could also create self-change contracts with themselves (Watson and Tharp, 1981).

PRACTICE TASK **8.6**

Use the checklist provided in Figure 8.1 to rate the last training program offered to your staff.

MAINTAINING NEW SKILLS

Another cluster of decisions that must be made concerns the maintenance of desired performance. Without attention to this important area, desired behaviors may drift downward. Maintenance will require arrangement of procedures to achieve this. Here, as in all other areas we have discussed, there are many alternatives to consider. Often nothing is done. That is, no attention is devoted to maintenance. A supervisor may simply hope that desired behaviors will be maintained without taking steps to ensure this. A second error is reliance on the influence of professional standards of performance; that is, a belief that social workers should want to maintain high levels of performance. (This is one version of the really-oughta-wanna belief [Mager and Pipe, 1970]). A third error is believing that arranging for maintenance of desired performance levels will be very time-consuming when, in fact, extending such efforts should in the long run save time as well as serve other important functions, such as maintaining staff morale and offering positive feedback concerning quality of service offered. Appropriate prompts and incentives will have to be provided to ensure that new skills are used (see Chapters 7 and 8). Feedback concerning success in achieving outcomes related to new skills offers one source of support for new competencies. Praise should also be provided. This will require monitoring of skills and outcomes achieved. A maintenance checklist is provided in Figure 8.2.

Appropriate cues are provided.	____ Yes	____ No
Needed tools are available.	____ Yes	____ No
Opportunities for regular practice are available.	____ Yes	____ No
Positive incentives for desired behaviors are offered.	____ Yes	____ No
Positive consequences for inappropriate behavior are withheld.	____ Yes	____ No
Use of new skills makes life easier.	____ Yes	____ No
Negative consequences for desired behaviors are minimized.	____ Yes	____ No

Figure 8.2   Maintenance Checklist

Sampling of behaviors and materials that you would like your workers to value should be arranged. For example, Hayes and Hawkins (1976) describe attempts to encourage students to seek out environments and materials that will enhance effectiveness and learning, such as subscribing to professional journals, joining professional organizations, participating in practice research, and taking an active role in influencing agency policy. One method used to increase interest in practice-research was to hold weekly meetings of students, faculty, and agency staff to discuss possible practice-research activities.

Identification of ways to shift responsibility for maintaining skills to line staff is usually easy after a clearly defined process has been established. Let us say, for example, that you review all cases every month to determine the percentage of cases in each caseload in which objectives are clearly identified. After this review procedure is established, responsibility for gathering information could be given to your workers. The checklists described in Chapter 3 can be used by staff to determine the percentage of steps they have satisfied in each case.

SUMMARY

Training will be required to enhance skill levels of staff. Important ingredients of training programs include clear identification of outcomes and related skills, tailoring of programs to individual competency levels of each participant, model presentation, practice opportunities both during training and on the job, constructive feedback, and prompts and incentives to support new skills.

Chapter 9

INTERPERSONAL
DECISION-MAKING SKILLS

Effective supervisors have effective interpersonal skills. The purpose of this chapter is to highlight required skills, to offer some useful rules of thumb for enhancing your interpersonal competencies, and to identify sources that offer more detailed descriptions. Effective supervision requires a wide range of interpersonal skills. You must offer rewarding feedback, handle emotional outbursts and complaints effectively, mediate conflicts that arise, respond to criticism, make and refuse requests, help workers find solutions to work-related interpersonal dilemmas, delegate responsibility, be persistent in the face of resistance, persuade others, build consensus, conduct effective meetings, anticipate and remove obstacles to communication, handle difficult people, and offer clear instructions.

Decisions must be made about how to handle troubling interpersonal situations as well as how to avoid when possible. You will have to decide how to pursue social goals related to successful supervisory performance. Examples of social goals include reaching agreement with a line worker concerning changes that should be made in his performance; reaching a satisfactory compromise with a higher-level administrator concerning feedback that you would like from her, encouraging effective staff behavior by supportive comments. You will have to make decisions about whether to use direct or indirect methods in given social situtations — for example, whether to take action to change a situation (a direct approach) or to change how you "frame" the situation (an indirect approach in which no action is taken). For instance, you may decide that an annoying behavior that you would like to change on the part of a secretary (for example, gum cracking at her desk) really doesn't matter (Lazarus and Launier, 1978). Effective social behavior avoids problematic situations and/or alters situations so that they are no longer problematic and at the same time offers a maximum of other positive consequences and a minimum of negative ones. Research clearly shows that social behavior involves a mutual influence process in which we influence each other. Lip service is often given to this important point, but in practice it is often forgotten. For example you may complain about a person's reactions toward you and place all blame on the other person without recognizing how your reactions contribute to the situation. We cannot not communicate. Whether your choose to or not, your reactions and self-presentation will influence others. Your work will be more satisfying if you are skilled in offering impressions to others that complement social goals you value.

PRACTICE TASK **9.1**

Give two examples of social situations in which you used a direct approach to achieve your goal.

PRACTICE TASK **9.2**

Give two examples of social situations in which you used an indirect approach to achieve your goals.

COMPONENTS OF EFFECTIVE
SOCIAL BEHAVIOR

The components of social behavior correspond to the ways in which things can go wrong. Goals, plans, and feedback are very important (Argyle et al., 1981). Behavior may be ineffective because people have inappropriate social goals in a situation, or because they have not identified their goals (Trower et at. 1978). Their goals may be appropriate, but they may fail to make plans or make inappropriate plans. Effective plans require effective problem-solving skills: (1) clear description of the situation; (2) description of alternatives; (3) selection of criteria to use to evaluate alternatives; (4) using these criteria to weigh the advantages and and disadvantages of each alternative; (5) choosing the best alternative; (6) trying this out; (7) evaluating the results; and (8) changing what you do in similar situations in the future based upon the effectiveness of your plan (D'Zurilla and Goldfried, 1971). Collection of additional information is often a critical first step in interpersonal problem solving. This will require caution in accepting reports about a situation at face value.

Social behavior may be ineffective because of lack of attention to feedback provided by others or distortion of feedback. Effective behavior is *situationally specific*; what will be effective in one situation may not be in another. This is why knowledge of rules about acceptable and unacceptable behavior in given situations is important. Many situations require special skills — skills that are somewhat unique to that situation. For example, conducting an employment interview requires skills that are somewhat different from those involved in having an enjoyable social conversation. Both verbal and nonverbal behaviors are important in our social behavior. Many studies have shown that verbal behavior carries more weight in influencing others than does verbal behavior; that is, *how* you say something is more important than *what* you say to others.

Rewardingness is one of the most important skills. People differ in how supportive they are of other people's behavior and how much they show liking rather than dislike of others. Effective behavior requires recognition of the situational specificity of social behavior. This will require knowledge of the rules and norms related to social behavior in given situations. For instance, there are gender differences in what will be effective in different situations. It has been demonstrated that women who sit at the head of a table are not as likely as are men to be perceived as the leader of a group (Porter and Geis, 1981). Other components of effective social behavior include self-presentation, the ability to take the role of others, and flexibility and creativity in drawing upon social skills.

PRACTICE TASK **9.3**

Give three examples of interpersonal situations that are of concern to you on the job and identify your goals in each.

Review your goals to see if they

(a) are specific,
(b) are achievable,
(c) consider your own values,
(d) consider the interests of others, and
(e) consider long-term as well as short-term consequences.

DIFFERENT SOURCES OF INFLUENCE

Effective social behavior requires knowledge about different sources of influence that can be successfully used in different situations.

According to French and Raven (1959), sources of influence include reward power (the ability to reward others), coercive power (the ability to punish others), expert power (others believe that you possess knowledge that is useful to them), referent power (influence based on people's liking you), and legitimate power (possessing influence to encourage others to comply because they believe they should). The relative advantages and disadvantages of coercive and reward power were discussed in Chapter 7. The higher others perceive your expert power to be, the more frequently they will solicit your advice. The greater is your referent power, the less you will have to rely on other sources of power. The distinction between supervision and consultation made by some writers (e.g., Munson, 1979) is based on different sources of power; consultation implies an equal balance of reward, coercive, and legitimate power in contrast to supervision, in which the supervisor holds higher reward, coercive, and legitimate power than does the worker.

Workers, supervisors, and higher-level administrators should clearly understand the bases of power at their disposal; their right to act (or not act) in certain situations. As Munson (1979:339) notes, falsely labeling a supervisory relationship as a consultative one,

> to make the process more palatable can lead to conflict, gradual isolation and lack of interaction when the worker learns that in many instances he does not have the freedom to act contrary to the supervisor's views.

We do not agree with Munson that possible conflicts in this area call for a separation of consultation and supervisory tasks between two different people; what is important is for involved parties to clearly distinguish between situations in which a consultative relationship is appropriate and those in which a supervisory relationship is appropriate. Relationships that involve different sources of power "feel different". If you and your staff share a high level of referent power, you and your workers will enjoy offering positive experiences to each other. If you rely on reward and coercive power, although the same quality of work may result, the shared feeling will be different.

PRACTICE TASK **9.4**

List the source(s) of influence you typically use with line staff.

PRACTICE TASK 9.5

List source(s) of influence your supervisor usually uses in exchanges with you.

THE IMPORTANCE OF
GOALS, PLANS, AND SKILLS

Your social encounters will be more positive if you can identify specific verbal and nonverbal behaviors that are related to achieving desired outcomes in specific situations. You should first decide what your goals are in a certain situation. Let us say that your supervisor repeatedly interrupts you during discussions you have with her. You may decide to do nothing. If you decide that you would like to change this pattern, you should first identify your goals in this situation and then review these to make sure they are attainable, will lead to positive short-term and long-term consequences, and will complement your personal values (Nezu and D'Zurilla, 1979). Possible goals in this situation might be: (1) to decrease interruption attempts; (2) to do so in a way that increases your self-esteem and self-respect as well as your supervisor's self-esteem and self-respect. Clear description of your goals will make it easier to scan them to make sure they are positive, attainable, and consider long-term as well as short-term consequences.

You may have to learn more effective ways to resist interruption such as repeating the last few words of your statement when an interruption attempt is made (Gambrill and Richey, forthcoming). Perhaps your skills in resisting interruption are already very good and you have used these without success. You will then have to select another approach such as discussing the matter with your supervisor, following the guidelines described later in this chapter for offering feedback. Be sure to select an appropriate time to discuss the topic. If you like your supervisor and, overall, enjoy the discussions you have with her, point this out first. You might say

> I enjoy our conversation and find them helpful (pause). These would be even more enjoyable to me if we could make one change (pause). I often feel that I don't get a chance to finish what I am saying before you reply. This upsets me because I lose my train of thought. I would appreciate it if you would let me finish what I am saying before you reply. This would make me feel that you are really interested in what I am saying and would make me feel more relaxed. Would you be willing to consider this?

This illustrates a five-step process of offering feedback (Agigian, 1982):
When . . . I feel . . . because . . . I would prefer . . . Because.

This conversation should be accompanied by matching nonverbal
behaviors. For example, the verbal message above would be diluted if
you have little eye contact when talking, or if you smile or giggle. A
request for a behavior change should be accompanied by direct eye
contact and a serious expression. This is not a humorous matter. Notice
that the person in our example requested a behavior change. If
achieving a behavior change is one of your goals in a situation, and you
have decided to discuss this with the person involved, be sure to make
the request. Many times, people never actually request a behavior
change. They often point out what they don't like and never ask for
what they *would* like, assuming (often incorrectly) that the other person
will know what is desired. (See also the section on offering feedback).
You may use the checklist in Figure 9.1 to review your goals, plans, and
actions in a given situation.

PRACTICE TASK **9.6**

Select an interpersonal situation of concern to you and briefly describe
this, including your goals. Then identify verbal and nonverbal
behaviors relevant to success in achieving your goals in this situation.

List several verbal and nonverbal behaviors that you should use in
pursuing these goals.

List several verbal and nonverbal behaviors that you should avoid in
pursuing these goals.

EXAMPLES OF IMPORTANT
SOCIAL COMPETENCIES

OFFERING FEEDBACK

The administrative, supportive, and educative roles of supervisors
require offering feedback to others. Heppner and Handley (1982) found
that when trainees perceived supervisors as frequently offering evaluative behaviors, they also viewed their supervisors as more expert,
attractive, and trustworthy. The quality of feedback offered will
influence your work satisfaction as well as that of your staff. Important
characteristics of helpful feedback include the following (Filley, 1975;
Brammer, 1973; Stuart, 1980):

— It should be descriptive rather than evaluative.

— It should refer to specific behaviors.

— It should focus on positives.

— Process rather than terminal language should be used. (It should concern events that can be changed.)

— It should be offered when people are most likely to receive it.

— It should be offered in an appropriate manner (see later discussion).

— It should be based on data that support it.

— It should be personalized (that is, of importance to the person receiving it rather than serving only your interests).

Feedback should be descriptive. It should describe behaviors and outcomes rather than use evaluative labels such as "dissatisfied," "bad," and "ineffective." Let us say that a worker's case recording is not up to date. You should first clearly identify what you would like; what your goals are. Let us say your goal is, in the most positive way possible, to increase the number of cases in which recording is up to

---

1. What were my goals in this situation? Were they appropriate?
2. Did I have a plan to achieve my goals? Was this appropriate?
3. What cues did I attend to during this interaction? Were they relevant or irrelevant? distracting or helpful?
4. Did I try to offer others a rewarding experience?
5. What did I say or not say that was helpful?
6. What did I say or not say that was unconstructive?
7. What expectations did I have of others in this situation?
8. What were my beliefs about *myself* in this situation?
9. Was my nonverbal behavior helpful or dysfunctional? (Identify specific nonverbal behaviors that occurred to often, too seldom, at the wrong time, in the wrong form, or were too stereotyped.)
10. Did I consider the perspective of others?
11. Did I follow the rules of this situation? If not, what specific rules did I violate?
12. Were there special skills required in this situation that I do not have?
13. Was my self-presentation appropriate? If not, how could this be improved?
14. Was I too controlling or too controlled?

SOURCE: Gambrill (1983: 158).

Figure 9.1 Troubleshooting Checklist

date. Note that, in addition to identifying a task-oriented goal, you have also set process goals — goals related to how the feedback is offered. You accept a definition of social competence that includes maintaining or enhancing positive feelings among participants, encouraging positive self-evaluative statements, as well as getting the job done. This will help you to personalize feedback (see discussion below) and to identify common interests. This attention to process as well as outcome goals will stand all parties in good stead on future occasions, when they can draw upon a "bank account" of positive shared events. There are, thus, practical as well as altruistic considerations in offering feedback in a positive manner; people are more likely to act upon feedback if it is provided in a way that protects and enhances self-esteem and self-interests. They are more likely to want to please people they like and so act in a manner to do so. A staff member who is asked in a positive way to increase the timeliness of her recording will be more likely to do so than is one who is asked in an inconsiderate fashion.

A common mistake made when offering feedback is to focus on negatives without recognizing positive aspects of the person's work. This will encourage a defensive attitude on the part of the recipient and is unfair in not recognizing accomplishments. It is unfair to ask people to change outcomes or behaviors if they have no influence over related factors. Perhaps case recording is not up-to-date because of inadequate secretarial help. This point is related to personalizing feedback. One component of offering personalized feedback is to explore obstacles that may exist, either personal or environmental, to acting in an expected way. Another aspect of offering personalized feedback is discussing interests that both you and the worker share for keeping records up-to-date. People are more likely to carry out expected behaviors if they understand and accept the rationale for doing so. This rationale should be noted early in the discussion, followed by an exploration of obstacles from the worker's point of view of what stands in the way of acting as expected. Obstacles, like competencies, are personal; people differ in their perceptions of these. Just because you do not view some event as an obstacle does not mean that a worker might not do so. Obstacles raised should be carefully appraised in terms of whether or not they indeed pose an obstacle and, if so, how this can be removed.

Knowledge about the worker's past record-keeping behavior may be helpful in reviewing obstacles and the potential for removing these, as well as for identifying incentives that could be offered. The flowchart in Figure 7.1 can serve as a useful guide to reviewing obstacles. Personalizing feedback is based on two important rules of thumb: (1) Think the best, not the worst, about people; and (2) consider the other person's perspective. The quality of your listening skills is a critical component of offering feedback (see e.g., Gambrill, 1983; Egan, 1982; Carkhuff and Anthony, 1979).

You must decide when to offer feedback. A time should be selected when people are most likely to be receptive to feedback. Times when workers are harried or tired should be avoided. Feedback should be based on data that support it. For example, have you actually examined this worker's records to see whether records are up-to-date? Requests for behavior change based on hearsay evidence should be avoided.

PRACTICE TASK 9.7

Describe two instances in which you liked the way you offered feedback to a worker. Write down what you said.

Review what you said against the criteria described in the text.

PRACTICE TASK 9.8

Describe two situations at work in which you were not happy about the feedback you offered.

Review your statements against the criteria described in the text. What should you have done differently?

REWARDINGNESS

Social psychologists who study interpersonal behavior stress the importance of rewardingness in our interactions — the extent to which we share our pleasure with and approval of others through our verbal and nonverbal behavior. Since our nonverbal behavior weighs heavily in terms of effects on others, it is especially important to occasionally check this if your interactions are not as positive as you would like them to be. Nonverbal behaviors associated with liking include (1) closer interpersonal distances; (2) touching; (3) forward lean; (4) facing others; (5) moderate body relaxation; (6) open body positions with arms unfolded; (7) welcoming facial expressions, such as smiling; (8) affirmative head nods; (9) a moderate amount of gesturing and animation and; (10) pleasant and supportive para-language that shows signs of interest in what others are saying, such as saying "um hum" (Schlenker, 1980: 257). If you do not offer such reactions to others, you are likely to be perceived as cold and as not liking others. We can all benefit at times by checking the level of the rewarding behaviors we

offer, such as direct eye contact and smiling, to make sure we offer
levels that facilitate positive encounters with others. It is especially
important to check this at times when you know from experience that
you tend to be less rewarding to others — for example, if you are tired
or overworked.

PRACTICE TASK **9.9**

Keep track for one day of the number of opportunities you took
advantage of to offer a pleasant experience to others, and record the
total.

PRACTICE TASK **9.10**

Note specific ways in which you could be more rewarding to others.

PRACTICE TASK **9.11**

What rules of thumb do you use about people that make your day
and their day brighter?

PRACTICE TASK **9.12**

What rules of thumb do you use about people that make your day
and their day dimmer?

NEGOTIATION SKILLS

Enjoyment of a supervisory role will require effective negotiation
skills, and some excellent guidelines are available describing components of successful negotiation. Fisher and Ury (1983) point out the
importance of identifying a common interest and focusing on this. This
will decrease the likelihood of defensive and other negative reactions.
How conflicts can be handled will depend, in part, on whether either or
both parties insist on an adversarial relationship. Outside mediators
may be needed to settle disputes in which adversarial relationships exist
and in which one or both parties are unwilling to communicate about
their differences and work toward a solution that is mutually acceptable.

PRACTICE TASK **9.13**

Write down strategies you have found helpful in reaching compromises with others.

AVOID GAME PLAYING

Supervisors, line staff, or higher-level administration may attempt to play games. "Games people play in supervision are concerned with the kinds of recurrent interactional incidents between supervisor and supervisee that have a payoff for one of the parties in the transaction" (Kadushin, 1968:23). As Kadushin points out, people play games because of the payoff. Thus, if someone at work is engaged in game playing, identify the payoffs involved. What is this person getting out of recurrent use of this pattern? What do you get out of it, if anything?

Potential sources of discomfort that may arise between supervisees and their supervisors and between supervisors and higher-level administration are well known (e.g., Kadushin, 1976). As Kadushin (1976:24) points out, "learning requires some frank admission of dependence on a teacher." It requires an admission that someone else knows more than you do. Students are dependent on supervisors for grades, which will in turn influence whether or not they achieve their professional goals. These sources of discomfort may be responsible for game playing. Lack of effective skills could also be responsible. People may or may not be aware that they are playing games. Kadushin (1968) offers an entertaining and useful discussion of various kinds of games supervisees use to manipulate demand levels, to redefine the relationship, to decrease power disparity and to control the situation. He also devotes attention to games supervisors play. As he points out, to omit reference to games initiated by supervisors would be unjust

in suggesting that they [supervisors] lack the imagination and capacity to devise their own counter-games. Supervisors play games out of felt threats to their position in the hierarchy, uncertainty about their authority, reluctance to use their authority, a desire to be liked, a need for the supervisees' approbation — and out of some hostility to supervisees that is inevitable in such a complex intimate relationship [Kadushin, 1968].

Kadushin notes that one of the classic supervisory games is "I wonder why you really said that?" (see also Hawthorne, 1975). Reasons for game playing mentioned above are also germane to games that may be played between supervisors and higher-level administrators.

Refusal to play is the most direct way to discourage game playing; after all, it does take two to play. Here, too, you will have to decide how not to play. You could introduce and reward another interactive pattern and withhold positive outcomes following "ploys," or if this is not effective, you could directly discuss the game.

STRESS MANAGEMENT SKILLS

Your stress management skills will influence the interpersonal decisions you make. Skill in regulating dysfunctional levels of anxiety, anger, or attraction are important. What you say to yourself is often directly related to what you feel. We can, for example, become very angry about a minor slight by ruminating about it — how insulting it really was, and so forth (see Greenburg, 1966). Alternatively, you could avoid becoming upset by dismissing the slight as unimportant, as not relevant to your goals, as not worth getting upset about. Here, too, helpful rules of thumb and questions are important to have at hand. Examples include the following:

— Consider the other person's viewpoint.

— It's not worth getting upset about.

— What is my goal here?

— Will getting upset help me accomplish my goal?

Effective time management skills will help you to moderate stress levels (see, e.g., Lakein, 1973; Scott, 1980).

Preparing for difficult encounters will help you handle these successfully. Let us say that you have decided to talk to your supervisor about a change you would like to make. You should practice what you will say and how you will handle anticipated difficult situations before you talk to your supervisor. Practice is very important in handling a difficult situation well. You may even wish to try out what you will say and do with another supervisor. If you can predict some reactions of your supervisor, you can prepare for these by practicing what you will do and say (or not do and say) when these take place. If there is a possibility that you might become more emotionally involved in this encounter than you would like, then you should also practice calming and task-focused statements such as "take it easy"; "stay calm"; and "what is my goal here?" (see for example, Bernstein and Borkovec, 1973; Walker, 1975).

For additional guidelines concerning social skills see Austin (1981), Burns (1980), Bower and Bower (1976), Donaldson (1980), Jakubowski and Lange (1978), Sundel and Sundel (1980), Morton et al. (1981), Strayhorn (1977), Tropman and Mills (1980), and Zander (1982).

SUMMARY

Your role as a supervisor will require a range of interpersonal skills, including offering constructive feedback, negotiating desired changes, avoiding problematic situations and handling complaints and criticisms. The quality of your stress management skills will influence the interpersonal decisions you make. Effective social behavior requires selection of appropriate social goals and plans for achieving these, accurate perception, and translation of social signals as well as effective verbal and nonverbal skills in specific situations. Effective social behavior is situationally specific; that is, what will be effective in one situation differs from what will be effective in other situations. Rewardingness — the extent to which you offer positive outcomes to others — is an especially important component of effective social behavior. Helpful rules of thumb — such as when in doubt, think the best rather than the worst about people — will encourage positive social exchanges.

Chapter 10

MAINTAINING SUCCESS AS
A SUPERVISOR

In order to be an effective supervisor, you must satisfy many constituencies: line staff, secretarial staff, consumers of service, and higher-lever administrators. You must also meet your own expectations. You must supervise others as well as deal with being supervised yourself and must do so within a resource system that is probably shrinking. Your skills as well as the skill levels of those with whom you interact, will influence the quality of your work, the quality of work you encourage in others, and your job satisfaction. Thus success and happiness as a supervisor involves a transactional process; if an unhappy state of affairs exists, the actions and inactions, the potentials and constraints of all involved parties should be explored to determine how more satisfying outcomes can be attained. The advantage of a transactional perspective is that you are rarely left without any source of influence to try to create change. A understanding of the transactional nature of the supervisory process as well as knowledge about how organizations function will be important contributors to your effectiveness.

THE ORGANIZATIONAL CONTEXT
OF SUPERVISION

The setting in which you work and the accuracy of your views of constraints and opportunities available within this will influence your effectiveness and satisfaction. If you look for a high or even moderate level of appreciation and recognition in your agency, you will probably be disappointed. (This does not mean that you cannot take steps to increase this. See Chapter 7.)

Complex organizations are notoriously inefficient distributors of appreciation and recognition. He who expects to receive in the bureaucratic milieu the emotional support that is only possible where relationships are intimate is doomed to suffer disappointment [Pruger, 1973: 29].

Careful distinctions must be drawn between behavior which is truely impersonal and that which is merely businesslike and humorless. [p. 30].

Appreciation of the kinds of feedback that are present and absent within your organization will be helpful in not responding to this in a personal manner.

An understanding of the legitimate authority and organizational enforcement in your agency is also necessary (Pruger, 1973). As Pruger points out, regulations are typically general, allowing considerable autonomy for workers and supervisors who take advantage of this range of discretion. An understanding of the boundaries of legitimate authority is important in recognizing the power you have to challenge informal procedures and to work toward implementation of new ones. If autonomy is lost in an organization, it is "because it was, perhaps unintentionally, given up, rather than because it was structurally precluded" (Pruger, 1973: 28). A vigilance in relation to both means and ends, and the extent to which each serves client as well as agency goals, is important. Goal displacement — a concentration on means rather than ends that serve clients — is common in social service agencies (e.g., Blau, 1955; Paulson, 1977). Participation in goal displacement rather than questioning of this, will decrease adequacy of services to clients as well as decrease job satisfaction. The guidelines presented in Chapter 7 will help you identify opportunities for change in your agency.

PRACTICE TASK 10.1

Identify a specific change you would like to make in your agency and write this down. Be specific.

How much discretion do you think you have to make this change?
____ a great detail   ____ some   ____ little   ____ none

Refer to Figure 7.2 and complete this in relation to the change described above. Were you correct in your estimate of how much discretion you have?

INTERACTIONS WITH
HIGHER-LEVEL ADMINISTRATORS

Other factors that will influence your effectiveness and the interpersonal situations you will face include the clarity of expectations of higher-level administrators, the match between these and what you think is appropriate, and the extent to which you assume initiative in clarifying vague expectations and improving the match between what exists and what you would like. The quality of your interpersonal skills will influence the quality of interactions you have with higher level administrators. (See Chapter 9.)

PRACTICE TASK 10.2

Answering the questions below will help you review expectations of higher-level administrators.

(1) What criteria does your supervisor use to evaluate your competence?
(2) Are these criteria clearly described?
(3) Are these criteria of direct relevance to offering high-quality services to clients?
(4) Have you participated in selection of these criteria?
(5) Do you consider these criteria important?
(6) What criteria do you think should be considered?

PRACTICE TASK 10.3

Answering the questions below will help you examine the nature of your relationship with higher-level administrators.

(1) Do you feel free to consult your supervisor about problems you have?
(2) Do you have regular meetings with higher-level administrators?
(3) Is time set aside in these meetings to discuss your concerns?
(4) Do you and your supervisor have an agreed-upon procedure for resolving differences that arise between you? If so, what is this?
(5) Would you describe your relationship with your supervisor as adversarial or congenial?
(6) What kinds of games (if any) do you and your supervisor play (e.g., both against the agency)?
(7) What kinds of feedback have you offered to your supervisor during the past six months?
(8) How accurately can you identify incentives of value to higher-level administrators?
(9) Do you have any control over such incentives?

Feedback from higher-level administrators offers one potential source of support for supervisors, as discussed below.

MAINTAINING EFFECTIVE
SUPERVISORY BEHAVIOR

Only if positive incentives are arranged will desired supervisory behaviors be maintained (see Chapter 7). What incentives can you use, and who will provide these? To answer these questions, you will first have to clearly identify outcomes of concern and arrange a way to monitor these. The planning chart in Figure 7.2 can be used to discover ways to rearrange antecedents and consequences related to desired outcomes. Potential sources of support for effective supervisory behavior include higher-level administrators line staff, other supervisors, professional in other agencies, clerical staff, and, self-reinforcement. Possible incentives that could be offered by each source are discussed below. You are urged to take the initiative in arranging supportive incentives and to be creative in identifying feasible incentives.

INCENTIVES FROM
HIGHER-LEVEL ADMINISTRATORS

What positive incentives do higher-level administrators offer you for expected achievements? Is recognition offered in any consistent fashion? In most agencies, no consistent positive feedback is offered for effective performance. Administrators should offer such feedback. If they do not, you should take the initiative in requesting feedback. Many items noted in Chapter 7 may function as incentives for supervisors as well as line workers and could be offered contingent on desired outcomes. Group contingencies could be used in which recognition is offered for achievement of "unit outcome." Group contingencies encourage mutual helping among workers as well as between staff and supervisors. Examples of outcomes of concern include percentage of cases in a unit in which objectives are clearly specified and percentage of cases in which clear progress indicators have been selected and monitored. Administrators together with supervisory and line staff could select a goal to focus on for a certain period, for example, six months. The first month's goal could be to gather baseline information concerning the percentage of cases in which clear objectives are identified. Positive incentives should be offered for collecting this information. A goal for the second month could be to increase by 10 percent the percentage of cases in which goals are clearly identified. Again, special recognition should be given to line staff and supervisors who meet this requirement.

Criterion levels can be increased over the following months. Examples of administrative incentives that could be offered to supervisors are listed below (see also Chapter 7).

— letter of commendation in personnel folder
— recognition in agency newsletter
— a personal letter of thanks
— freedom to take on individual cases
— extra clerical help
— access to desired opportunity
— a free lunch

Such arrangements may sound contrived, and they are. They are arranged to encourage effective supervisory and staff performance. The point is that if expected behaviors do not occur, you have a choice of only four alternatives: You can ignore the situation; you can use exhortation; you can use punishment; or you can encourage more effective behavior by offering opportunities for skill acquisition and provide cues and positive incentives for desired behaviors and outcomes. The last alternative is the most effective option (see Chapter 7).

PRACTICE TASK **10.4**

List the positive incentives you receive from higher-level administrators, and note after each what these are offered for.

List the negative incentives you receive from higher-level administrators, and after each note what these are offered for.

PRACTICE TASK **10.5**

Indicate some incentives you would like to receive more frequently from higher-level administrators.

PRACTICE TASK **10.6**

Write down one example of a group contingency that could be used in your agency.

FEEDBACK FROM PROFESSIONALS
IN OTHER AGENCIES

How often have you taken the time to praise someone in another agency for an especially fine piece of work? How often do you take the time to place such positive feedback in written form? All too often we only *think* about offering positive feedback. How often have you received a written note of praise from a staff member in another agency for help you extended or an outcome you achieved? You could increase positive feedback by offering a model of such feedback yourself; that is, by calling or writing staff in other agencies to offer praise for specific achievements or help offered. You can decrease the time involved in offering such feedback by making sure you have required materials readily available — note cards, envelopes, stamps, or official agency stationary. These notes do not have to be lengthy. Be sure to be specific about the reason for your praise. Praise for *specific* outcomes or behavior is more likely to result in an increase or maintenance of valued behaviors. Examples of outcomes or behaviors that warrant praise include the following:

— help in locating a needed resource

— speedily returning telephone calls

— timely return of requested written information

— initiation of a needed program

— receipt of a grant

INCENTIVES FROM LINE STAFF

Line staff provide another source of incentives for example, in terms of approval. If valued supervisory behaviors do not occur, contingencies they offer should be examined. Let us say that staff complain that you do not offer enough feedback about procedures used. Perhaps staff offer little thanks or approval for your feedback, or perhaps they punish your efforts. Under these circumstances, your offers of help will decrease. Incentives your staff could offer may include taking you out to lunch, giving you a subscription to a favorite magazine or journal, or sending a letter of praise about you to a higher-level administrator. The more specific your staff can be in clearly describing what they would like you to do more or less of, the more effective they can be in encouraging desired changes. Here, too, you do not have to await the initiation of others; you can take the initiative by informing workers that it would be helpful if they would clearly describe changes they would like.

You can exert an important influence by modeling behaviors you would like to encourage. For example, the more specific you are when offering praise or criticism, the more opportunities staff have to acquire such skills. If you complain that your workers are disheartened and complain often, and if you yourself often complain about how awful the system is, you are encouraging complaining behavior.

PRACTICE TASK 10.7

List incentives you would like to receive more often from line staff. Describe two ways you could increase the likelihood of receiving these.

FEEDBACK FROM OTHER SUPERVISORS

We have been surprised by the lack of sharing among social workers, including supervisors, in terms of helpful procedures and suggestions for resolving concerns. Lack of sharing removes one possible source of support for effective practice — recognition from peers. It also decreases the overall achievement of an agency, since effective methods are not shared with other staff members. Regular meetings among supervisory staff could be arranged and supervisors encouraged to identify needed changes and to share possible ways to achieve them. Since many supervisory problems are common for all supervisors, solutions proposed should benefit all participants. In addition to verbal support, other incentives could be planned, such as having lunch at a favorite spot if each supervisor achieves an agreed-upon outcome.

PRACTICE TASK 10.8

Describe two opportunities you missed during the past two weeks to offer positive feedback to another supervisor.

FEEDBACK FROM CLERICAL STAFF

What type of feedback do clerical staff, line staff, and supervisors offer to each other? Is this mostly positive or mostly negative? You may have to prompt feedback from clerical staff by requesting it concerning changes they would like to see. Examples of incentives clerical staff could offer to supervisors include the following:

— thanks for giving them sufficient time to complete a task

—   thanks for keeping crisis requests to a minimum

—   keeping vague complaints to a minimum

PRACTICE TASK 10.9

List three kinds of positive feedback you could offer more frequently to clerical staff.

SELF-REINFORCEMENT

Self-reinforcement provides a valuable source of feedback. You could select a change you would like to make and offer yourself a reward if this is accomplished. Criteria allowing you to determine whether your goal is achieved should be clearly described. For example, you could agree that if goals are identified in each worker's caseload for 38% of the families by the end of three weeks, you will visit a museum you have wanted to explore. In some cases, achieving the goal may be sufficiently rewarding to maintain behavior. The skills you develop in making agreements with yourself will be valuable in helping staff to select clear objectives and progress indicators and design effective contingencies. In addition to external rewards, such as a visit to a museum or attending a training session, you should also offer yourself positive self-statements (see Chapter 7).

PRACTICE TASK 10.10

Create a written agreement with yourself concerning a change you would like to make. Be sure to select one that is obtainable, measurable, and meaningful. Select a reward you could offer yourself. Write down the agreement on the form in Figure 10.1.

Date: _____ Name: _____

If I _____

_____

_____

by (date) _____,

then I _____

_____

Figure 10.1 Self-Change Agreement

PRACTICE TASK 10.11

Write down four examples of positive self-statements you offered to yourself during the past week.

Review these to determine whether they meet the following criteria:

(a)   They refer to specific accomplishments.
(b)   They do not contain any put-downs (e.g., I did _____, *but . . .*).
(c)   They were believable to you.
(d)   They made you feel better.

SUMMARY

Your success and happiness as a supervisor will require attention to incentives you offer to yourself for effective behavior as well as incentives offered by higher-level administrators, line staff, clerical staff, and other supervisors. An understanding of constraints and possibilities within your agency will help you identify opportunities for helpful changes that you can make. Only if positive incentives are arranged for behaviors you would like to maintain will these behaviors continue. It is thus important that you take the initiative in identifying and arranging positive incentives for effective behaviors on an ongoing basis.

REFERENCES

Advisory Committee on child Development, Assembly of Behavioral and Social Sciences (1976) Toward a National Policy For Children and Families. Washington, DC: National Academy of Sciences.

AGIGIAN, H. (1982) Personal communication.

ARGYLE, M., A. FURNHAM, and J. A. Graham (1981) Social Situations. Cambridge: Cambridge University Press.

AUSTIN, M. J. (1981) Supervisory Management for the Human Services. Englewood Cliffs, NJ: Prentice-Hall.

BAKER, T., S. CORNELIUS, J. KELLY, D. W. BRITTON, R. ELVERHOY, and G. HOSHINO (1981) "Making peace with the computer." Public Welfare 39.

BAUM, C. G., R. FOREHAND, and L. E. ZEGIOB (1979) "A review of observer reactivity in adult-child interactions." Journal of Behavioral Assessment 1: 167-178.

BELLACK, A. S. (1979) "A critical appraisal of strategies for assessing social skill." Behavioral Assessment 1: 157-176.

——— R. ROSENSKY, and J. SCHWARTZ (1974) "A comparison of two forms of self-monitoring in a behavioral weight reduction program." Behavior Therapy 5: 523-530.

BERNSTEIN, D. A. and T. D. BORKOVEC (1973) Progressive Relaxation: A Manual for the Helping Professions. Champaign, IL: Research Press.

BERNSTEIN, D. A. and M. T. NIETZEL (1980) Introduction to Clinical Psychology. New York: McGraw-Hill.

BLAU, P. M. (1955) The Dynamics of Bureaucracy. Chicago: University of Chicago Press.

BLOOM, M. and J. FISHER (1982) Evaluating Practice: Guidelines for the Accountable Professional. Englewood Cliffs, NJ: Prentice-Hall.

BOEHM, B. (1962) "An assessment of family adequacy in protective cases." Child Welfare 41: 12.

BOLIN, D. C., and L. KIVENS (1974) "Evaluation in a community mental health center." Evaluation 2: 26-35.

BOMMER, M., G. GOODGION, V. PEASE, and R. ZMUD (1977) "Development of an information system for the Child Abuse and Neglect Service System." Community Mental Health Journal 13: 333-342.

BOWER, S. A. and G. H. BOWER (1976) Asserting Yourself. Reading, MA: Addison-Wesley.

BOYD, L. H., Jr., M. CLARK, and S. P. HANSON (1980) "A worker-centered information system." Evaluation Review 4: 637-644.

BRAMMER, L. (1973) The Helping Relationship: Process and Skills. Englewood Cliffs, NJ: Prentice-Hall. (See also 2nd ed., 1979.)

BREKSTAD, A. (1966) "Factors influencing the reliability of anamnestic recall." Child Development 37: 603-612.

BRIELAND, D. (1959) An Experimental Study in the Selection of Adoptive Parents at Intake. New York: Child Welfare League of America.

BROCKWAY, B. S. et al. (1977) "Training and evaluation of behavior therapists: methods and issues." Symposium presented at the Eleventh Annual Convention of the Association For Advancement of Behavioral Therapy, Atlanta, December.

BURNS , D. D. (1980) Feeling Good: The New Mood Therapy. New York: Morrow.

BURT, M. R. and R. R. BALYEAT (1977) A Comprehensive Emergency Services System for Neglected and Abused Children. New York: Vantage Press.

CARKHUFF, R. R. and W. A. ANTHONY (1979) The Skills of Helping. Amherst, MA: Human Resource Development Press.

CARTER, R. D. and E. J. THOMAS (1973) "Modification of problematic marital communication using corrective feedback and instruction." Behavior Therapy 4: 100-109.

CIMINERO, A. R., L. E. GRAHAM, and J. L. JACKSON (1977) "Reciprocal reactivity: response-specific changes in independent observers." Behavior Therapy 8: 48-56.

CLARK, F. W., M. L. ARKAVA, and Associates. (1979) The Pursuit of Competence in Social Work. San Francisco: Jossey-Bass.

CLARK, M., L. S. MILLER, and R. PRUGER (1980) "Treating clients fairly: equity in the distribution of in-home supportive services." Journal of Social Service Research 4: 47-60.

Cysis-Data Newsletter (1982) vol. 3, no. 1 (June).

——— (1981) vol. 2, no. 1 (April): 1, 7.

DAVISON, G. C. and R. B. STUART (1975) "Behavior therapy and civil liberties." American Psychologist 30: 755-763.

DOMASH, M. A., J. F. SCHNELLE, E. L. STROMATT, A. F. CARR, L. D. LARSON, R. E. KIRSHNER, and T. R. RISLEY (1980) "Police and prosecution systems: an evaluation of a police-criminal case preparation program." Journal of Applied Behavior Analysis 13: 397-406.

DONALDSON L. (1980) Behavioral Supervision: Practical Ways to Change Unsatisfactory Behavior and Increase Productivity. Reading, MA: Addison-Wesley.

D'ZURILLA, T. and M. GOLDFRIED (1971) "Problem solving and behavior modification." Journal of Abnormal Psychology 78: 107-126.

EGAN, G. (1982) The Skilled Helper: A Model for Systematic Helping and Interpersonal Relating. Monterey, CA: Brooks/Cole.

EMLEN, A.C. J. LAHTI, G. DOWNS, A. McKAY, and S. DOWNS (1977) Overcoming Barriers to Planning for Children in Foster Care. Portland, OR: Regional Research Institute For Human Services.

EMLEN, A. C. and Staff (1976) Barriers to Planning for Children in Foster Care, vol. 1. Portland, OR: Regional Research Institute for Human Services.

EVANS, I. M. and R. O. NELSON (1977) "Assessment of child behavior problems," in A. R. Ciminero et al. (Eds.) Handbook of Behavioral Assessment. New York: John Wiley.

FANSHEL, D. and E. B. SHINN (1978) Children in Foster Care: A Longitudinal Investigation. New York: Columbia University Press.

FIELDING, L. T., E. ERRICKSON and B. BETTIN (1971) "Modification of staff behavior: a brief note." Behavior Therapy 2: 550-553.

FILLEY, A. C. (1975) Interpersonal Conflict Resolution. Glenview, Ill: Scott, Foresman.

FISHER, R. and W. URY (1983) Getting to Yes: Reaching Agreement Without Giving In. New York: Penguin.

FIXEN, D. L., E. L. PHILLIPS, and M. M. WOLF (1972) 'Achievement Place: the reliability of self-reporting and peer reporting and their effects on behavior." Journal on Applied Behavior Analysis 5: 19-30.

FRENCH, J. R. P., Jr. and B. RAVEN (1959) "The bases of social power," in D. Cartwright (ed.) Studies in Social Power. Ann Arbor: University of Michigan, Institute For Social Research.

GAEL, S. (1983) Job Analysis: A Guide to Assessing Work Activities. San Francisco: Jossey-Bass.

GAGNE, R. M. (1977) The Conditions of Learning. New York: Holt, Rinehart and Winston.

GAMBRILL, E. (1983) Casework: A Competency Based Approach. Englewood Cliffs, NJ: Prentice-Hall.

——— and C. A. RICHEY (forthcoming) Take Charge of Your Social Life. Belmont, CA: Wadsworth.

GAMBRILL, E. D. and T. J. STEIN (1978) Supervision in Child Welfare: A Training Manual. Berkeley: University of California, Extension Publications.

GAMBRILL, E. D., E. J. THOMAS, and R. D. CARTER (1971) "Procedure for sociobehavioral practice in open settings." Social Work 16: 51-62.

GILLEN, R. W. and R. G. HEIMBERG (1980) "Social skills training for the job interview: review and prospectus," in M. Hersen et al. Progress in Behavior Modification, vol. 10. New York: Academic.

GOCKEL, G. L. (1967) "Social work as a career choice," in E. Schwartz (ed.) Manpower and Social Welfare: Research Perspectives. New York: National Association of Social Workers.

GOLAN, N. (1969) "How caseworkers decide: a study of the association of selected applicant factors with worker decision in admission services." Social Service Review 43: 289-296.

GOLDFRIED, M. R. (1980) "Toward the delineation of therapeutic change principles." American Psychologist 35: 991-999.

GOLDHAMMER, R. (1969) Clinical Supervision. New York: Holt, Rinehart and Winston.

GOLDSTEIN, H. (1973) Social Work Practice: A Unitary Approach. Columbia: University of South Carolina Press.

GOLDSTEIN, J., A. FREUD, and A. J. SOLNIT (1973) Beyond the Best Interests of the Child. New York: Free Press.

GOTTLIEB, B. H. [ed.] (1981) Social Networks and Social Support. Beverly Hills, CA: Sage.

GOTTMAN, J. M. and S. R. LEIBLUM (1974) How To Do Psychotherapy and Evaluate It: A Manual for Beginners. New York: Holt, Rinehart and Winston.

GRAY, J. J. (1974) "Methods of training psychiatric residents in individual behavior therapy." Journal of Behavior Therapy and Experimental Psychiatry 5: 19-26.

GREENBURG, D. (1966) How To Make Yourself Miserable. New York: Random House.

GRUBER, A. R. (1978) Children in Foster Care: Destitute, Neglected . . . Betrayed. New York: Human Sciences Press.

HART, G.M. (1982) The Process of Supervision. Baltimore: University Park Press.

HARTSHORNE, H. and M. A. MAY (1928) Studies in the Nature of Character. I. Studies in Deceit. New York: MacMillan.

HAWTHORNE, L. (1975) "Games supervisors play." Social Work 20: 179-183.

HAYES, L. A. (1976) "The use of group contingencies for behavioral control: a review." Psychological Bulletin 83: 628-648.

HAYES, S. C. and N. CAVIOR (1977) "Multiple tracking and the reactivity of self-monitoring. I. Negative behaviors." Behavior Therapy 8: 819-831.

HAYES, S. C. and R. P. HAWKINS (1976) "Behavioral administration of analytic training programs: a beginning," pp. 85-112 in S. Yen and R. W. McIntire (eds.) Teaching Behavior Modification. Kalamazoo, MI: Behaviordelia.

HECK, E. T. and A. R. GRUBER (1976) Treatment Alternatives Project. Boston: Children's Service Association.

HELFER, R. E. and R. SCHMIDT (1976) "The community-based child abuse and neglect program," in R.E. Helfer and C.H. Kempe (eds.) Child Abuse and Neglect: The Family and the Community. Cambridge, MA: Ballinger.

HEPPNER, P. P. and P. HANDLEY (1982) "The relationship between supervisory behaviors and perceived supervisor expertness, attractiveness or trustworthiness." Counselor Education and Supervision 22: 37-46.

HERBERT, E. W. and D. M. BAER (1972) "Training parents as behavior modifiers: self-recording of contingent attention." Journal of Applied Behavior Analysis 5: 139-149.

HOBBS, N. (1975) The Futures of Children. San Francisco: Jossey-Bass.

IVY, A. and J. AUTHIER (1978) Microcounseling: Innovations in Interviewing, Counseling, Psychotherapy and Psychoeducation. Springfield, IL: Thomas.

IWATA, B. A., J. S. BAILEY, K. M. BROWN, T. J. FOSHEE, and M. ALPERN (1976) "A performance based lottery to improve residential care and training by institutional staff." Journal of Applied Behavior Analysis 9:417-431.

JAKUBOWSKI, P. and A. J. LANGE (1978) The Assertive Option: Your Rights and Responsibilities. Champaign, IL: Research Press.

JANOFF-BULMAN, R. (1979) "Characterological versus behavioral self-blame: inquiries into depression and rape." Journal of Personality and Social Psychology 37: 1798-1809.

JAYARATNE, S. and R. L. LEVY (1979) Empirical Clinical Practice. New York: Columbia University Press.

JENKINS, S. and E. NORMAN, (1975) Beyond Placement: Mothers View Foster Care. New York: Columbia University Press.

JENKINS, S. and M. SAUBER (1966) Paths to Child Placement. New York: Community Council of New York.

JOHNSON, S. M. and O. D. BOLSTAD (1975) "Reactivity to home observation: a comparison of audio-recorded behavior with observers present or absent." Journal of Applied Behavior Analysis 8: 181-185.

JOHNSON, S. M. and G. WHITE (1971) "Self-observation as an agent of behavior change." Behavior Therapy 2: 488-497.

JONES, M. L. (1977) "Aggressive adoption: a program's effect on a child welfare agency." Child Welfare 56: 401-407.

KADUSHIN, A. (1976) Supervision in Social Work. New York: Columbia University Press.

——— (1968) "Games people play in supervision." Social Work 13: 23-32.

KANFER, F. H. and J. S. PHILLIPS (1969) "A survey of current behavior therapies and a proposal for classification," in C. M. Franks (ed.) Behavior Therapy: Appraisal and Status. New York: McGraw-Hill.

KAZDIN, A. (1977) The Token Economy: A Review and Evaluation. New York: Plenum.

——— (1974) "Self-monitoring and behavior change," in M. J. Mahoney and C. E. Thoresen (eds.) Self-Control: Power to the Person. Monterey, CA: Brooks/Cole.

KENNISTON, K. and the Carnegie Council on Children. (1977) All Our Children: The American Family Under Pressure. New York: Harcourt Brace Jovanovich.

KIFER, R. E., M. A. LEWIS, D. R. GREEN, and E. L. PHILLIPS (1974) "Training predelinquent youths and their parents to negotiate conflict situations." Journal of Applied Behavior Analysis 7: 357-364.

KIRESUK, T. J. and G. GARWICK (1975) "Basic goal attainment scaling procedures," pp. 388-401 in B. R. Compton and B. Galaway (eds.) Social work processes. Homewood, IL: Dorsey.

KIRESUK, T. J. and R. E. SHERMAN (1968) "Goal attainment scaling: a general method for evaluating comprehensive community mental health programs." Community Mental Health Journal 4:443-453.

KURTZ, P. D. (1976) "A systematic supervisory procedure for child care training." Child Care Quarterly 5: 9-18.

LAKEIN, A. (1973) How To Get Control of Your Time and Your Life. New York: New American Library.

LAMBERT, M. J. (1980) "Research and supervisory process," in A. K. Hess (ed.) Psychotherapy Supervision: Theory, Research and Practice. New York: John Wiley.

——— S. S. DeJULIO, and D. M. STEIN (1978) "Therapist interpersonal skills: process, outcome, methodological considerations and recommendations for future research." Psychological Bulletin 85: 467-489.

LAPOUSE, R. and M. A. MONK (1958) "An epidemiologic study of behavior characteristics in children." American Journal of Public Health 48: 1134-1144.

LAZARUS, R. S. and R. LAUNIER (1978) "Stress-related transactions between person and environment," in L.A. Pervin and M. Lewis (eds.) Perspectives in Interactional Psychology. New York: Plenum.

LINEHAN, M. M. (1977) Issues in behavioral interviewing, pp. 30-51 in J. D. Cone and R. P. Hawkins (eds.) Behavioral Assessment: New Directions in Clinical Psychology. New York: Brunner/Mazel.

LIPINSKI, D. P., J. L. BLACK, and R. O. NELSON (1975) "Influence of motivational variables on the reactivity and reliability of self-recording." Journal of Consulting and Clinical Psychology 43: 637-646.

LIPTON, D. N. and R. D. NELSON (1980) "The contribution of initiation behavior to dating frequency." Behavior Therapy 11: 59-67.

LOEBER, R. (1971) "Engineering the behavioral engineer." Journal of Applied Behavior Analysis 4: 321-326.

LOFTUS, E. (1979) Eyewitness Testimony. Cambridge, MA: Harvard University.

LORIAN, R. P., E. L. COWEN, and R. A. CALDWELL (1974) "Problem types of children referred to a school-based mental health program: identification and outcome." Journal of Consulting and Clinical Psychology. 42: 491-496.

LOVETT, S. B., C. P. BOSMAJIAN, L. W. FREDERIKSEN, and J. P. ELDER (1983) "Monitoring professional service delivery. An organizational level intervention." Behavior Therapy 14: 170-171.

MADISON, B. Q. (1977) "Changing directions in child welfare services," in F. Sobey (ed.) Changing Roles in Social Work Practice. Philadelphia: Temple University Press.

MAGER, R. F. (1972) Goal Analysis. Belmont, CA: Fearon.

—— (1962) Preparing Instructional Objectives. Belmont, CA: Fearon.

—— and P. PIPE (1970) Analyzing Performance Problems. Belmont, CA: Fearon.

MAHONEY, M. J. and K. MAHONEY (1976) Permanent Weight Control. New York: Norton.

MALETSKY, B. M. (1974) "Behavior recording as treatment: a brief note." Behavior Therapy 5: 107-111.

MARTIN, G. L. (1972) "Teaching operant technology to psychiatric nurses, aides, and attendants," in F. W. Clark et al. Implementing Behavior Programs for schools and clinics. Champaign, IL: Research Press.

MECH, E. W. (1970) "Decision analysis in foster care practice," pp. 26-51 in H. D. Stone (ed.) Foster Care in Question. New York: Child Welfare League of America.

MILLER, L. and R. PRUGER (1979) "The two activities of social services: maintenance and people changing." University of California, Berkeley. (unpublished)

MISCHEL, W. (1968) Personality and Assessment. New York: John Wiley.

MONTEGAR, C. A., D. H. REID, C. H. MADSEN, and M. D. EWELL (1977) "Increasing institutional staff-to-resident interactions through in-service training and supervisory approval." Behavior Therapy 8: 533-540.

MORTON, J. C., C. A. RICHEY, and M. KELLETT (1961) Building Assertive Skills. St. Louis, MO: C.V. Mosby.

MUNSON, C. E. (1981) "Style and structure in supervision." Journal of Education for Social Work 17: 65-72.

—— (1979) "Authority and social work supervision: an emerging model," in C. E. Munson (ed.) Social Work Supervision: Classic Statements and Critical Issues. New York: Free Press.

MUSLIN, H. L., R. J. THURNBLAD, and G. MESCHEL (1981) "The fate of the clinical interview: an observational study." American Journal of Psychiatry 138: 822-825.

NELSON, R. O., D. P. LIPINSKI, and J. L. BLACK (1975) "The effects of expectancy on the reactivity of self-recording." Behavior Therapy 6: 373-349.

NEZU, A. and T. J. D'ZURILLA (1979) "An experimental evaluation of the decision-making process in social problem solving." Cognitive Therapy and Research 3: 269-277.

NISBETT, R. and L. ROSS (1980) Human Inference: Strategies and Shortcomings of Social Judgment. Englewood Cliffs, NJ: Prentice-Hall.

Office of Human Development, Children's Bureau (1976) Child Welfare in 25 States: An Overview. DHEW Publication (OHD) 76-30090. Washington, DC: Department of Health, Education and Welfare.

—— (1975) Child Abuse and Neglect: The Problem and Its Management, vol. 3. DHEW Publication (OHD) 75-30075. Washington, DC: Department of Health, Education and Welfare.

Office of Program Evaluation (1977) Placement in Foster Care: Issues and Concerns. Oakland, CA: County of Alameda.

PANYAN, M., H. BOOZER, and N. MORRIS (1970) "Feedback to attendants as a reinforcer for applying operant techniques." Journal of Applied Behavior Analysis 3: 1-4.

PATTERSON, E. T., J. C. GRIFFIN, and M. C. PANYAN (1976) "Incentive maintenance of self-help skill training programs for non-professional personnel." Journal of Behavior Therapy and Experimental Psychiatry 7: 249-253.

PATTERSON, R., C. COOKE, and R. P. LIBERMAN (1972) "Reinforcing the reinforcers: a method of supplying feedback to nursing personnel." Behavior Therapy 3: 444-446.

PAULSON, R. I. (1977) "A behavioral view of goal displacement in a social welfare agency." DSW dissertation. University of California, Berkeley.

PEDALINO, E. and V. GAMBOA (1974) "Behavior modification and absenteeism: intervention in one industrial setting." Journal of Applied Psychology 59: 694-698.

PELTON, L. H. (1981) "Child abuse and neglect and protective intervention in Mercer County, New Jersey," in L.H. Pelton (ed.) The Social Context of Child Abuse and Neglect. New York: Human Sciences Press.

PERLMAN, H. H. (1979) Relationship: The Heart of Helping. Chicago: University of Chicago Press.

PETERSON, G. L., A. E. HOUSE, and H. F. ALFORD (1975) "Self-monitoring: accuracy and reactivity in a patient's recording of three clinically targeted behaviors." Presented at the annual meeting of the Southeastern Psychological Association, Atlanta, March.

PETTES, D. E. (1979) Staff and Student Supervision: A Task Centered Approach. London: Allen & Unwin.

PHILLIPS, M. H., A. W. SHYNE, E. A. SHERMAN, and B. L. HARING (1971) Factors Associated with Placement Decisions in Child Welfare. New York: Child Welfare League of America.

PIKE, V., S. DOWNS, A. EMLEN, G. DOWNS, and D. CASE (1977) Permanent Planning for Children in Foster Care: A Handbook for Social Workers. Portland, OR: Regional Research Instistute For Human Services, Portland State University.

PINKSTON, E. M., J. L. LEVITT, G. R. GREEN, N. L. LINSK, and T. L. RZEPNICKI (1982) Effective Social Work Practice: Advanced Techniques for Behavioral Interventions with Individuals, Families and Institutional Staff. San Francisco: Jossey-Bass.

POLANSKY, N. A., C. HALLY, and N. F. POLANSKY (1975) Profile of Neglect: A Survey of the State of Knowledge of Child Neglect. Washington, DC: Department of Health, Education and Welfare, Public Services Administration.

POMERLEAU, O. F., P. H. BOBROVE, and R. H. SMITH (1973) "Rewarding psychiatric aides for the behavioral improvement of assigned patients." Journal of Applied Behavior Analysis 6: 383-390.

PORTER, N. and F. GEIS (1981) "Women and nonverbal leadership cues: when seeing is not believing," in C. Mayo and N. M. Henley (eds.) Gender and Nonverbal Behavior. New York: Springer-Verlag.

PRUGER, R. (1973) "The good bureaucrat." Social Work 18, 4: 26-32.

Public Services Administration (1973) Protective Services for Abused and Neglected Children and Their Families. Washington, DC: Department of Health, Education and Welfare.

QUAY, H. C. and D. R. PETERSON (1967) Manual for the Behavior Problem Checklist. Champaign: University of Illinois, Children's Research Center.

QUAY, H. C. and J. S. WERRY (1972) Psychopathological Disorders of Childhood. New York: John Wiley.

QUILITCH, H. R. (1978) "Using a simple feedback procedure to reinforce the submission of written suggestions by mental health employees." Journal of Organizational Behavior Management 1:115-163.

———(1975) "A comparison of three staff-management procedures." Journal of Applied Behavior Analysis 8: 59-66.

RAPP, C. A. (1982) "Effect of the availability of family support services on decisions about child placement." Social Work Research and Abstracts 18: 21-27.

RINN, R. C. and J. C. VERNON (1975) "Process evaluation of outpatient treatment in a community mental health center." Journal of Behavior Therapy and Experimental Psychiatry 6: 5-12.

ROBBINS, L. C. (1963) "The accuracy of parental recall of aspects of child development and child-rearing practice." Journal of Abnormal and Social Psychology 66: 261-270.

ROSENBERG, M., B. C. GLUECK, and C. F. STROEBEL (1967) "The computer and the clinical decision process." American Journal of Psychiatry, 124: 595-599.

ROSSI, P.H. (1982) Evaluation: A Systematic Approach. Beverly Hills, CA: Sage.

ROTTER, J. B. (1966) "Generalized expectancies for internal versus external control of reinforcement." Psychological Monographs 80, 1 (whole no. 609).

RUNYAN, D. K., C. L. GOULD, D. C. TROST, and F. A. LODA (1982) "Determinants of foster care placement for the maltreated child." Child Abuse and Neglect: The International Journal 6: 343-350.

SCHLENKER, B. R. (1980) Impression Management: The Self-Concept, Social Identity and Interpersonal Relations. Monterey, CA: Brooks/Cole.

SCHNELLE, J. F. (1974) "A brief report on invalidity of parent evaluations of behavior change." Journal of Applied Behavior Analysis 7: 341-343.

SCHOECH, D. and L.L. SCHKADE (1980) "Computers helping caseworkers: decision support systems." Child Welfare 59: 566-575.

SCHOPLER, E. and J. LOFTIN (1969) "Thought disorders in parents of psychotic children: a function of test anxiety." Archives of General Psychiatry 20: 174.

SCHWARTZ, A. and I. GOLDIAMOND (1975) Social Casework: A Behavioral Approach. New York: Columbia University Press.

SCOTT, D. (1980) How To Put More Time in Your Life. New York: Signet.

SHEAFER, B. W. and L. E. JENKINS (1982) Quality Field Instruction in Social Work. New York: Longman.

SHINN, E. G. (1969) "Is placement necessary? An experimental study of agreement among caseworkers in making foster care decisions. Ph.D. dissertation, Columbia University.

SHYNE, A. W. (1969) The Need for Foster Care. New York: Child Welfare League of America.

SKOLNICK, A. (1978) The Intimate Environment: Exploring Marriage and the Family. Boston: Little, Brown.

STEIN, T. J. (1982) Social Work Practice in Child Welfare. Englewood Cliffs NJ: Prentice-Hall.

——— (1974) "A content analysis of social caseworker and client interaction in foster care." DSW dissertation, University of California, Berkeley.

——— and E. D. GAMBRILL (1977) "The Alameda Project: two-year report." Social Service Review 51: 502-513.

STEIN, T. J. and T. L. RZEPNICKI (forthcoming) Decision Making in Child Welfare: Intake and Planning. Kluwer-Nijhoff.

——— (1983a) Decision Making at Child Welfare Intake: A Handbook for Practitioners. New York: Child Welfare League of America.

———— (1983b) "Decision making in child welfare: current issues and future directions," in B. McGowan and W. Meezan, (eds.) Child Welfare: Current Dilemmas-Future Directions. Itasca, IL: F.E. Peacock.

STEIN, T. J., E. D. GAMBRILL, and K. T. WILTSE (1978) Children in Foster Homes: Achieving Continuity of Care. New York: Praeger.

STOKES, T. F. and D. M. BAER (1977) "An implicit technology of generalization." Journal of Applied Behavior Analysis 10: 349-367.

STRAYHORN, J. M. (1977) Talking It Out: A Guide to Effective Communication and Problem Solving. Champaign, IL: Research Press.

STUART, R. B. (1980) Helping Couples Change: A Social Learning Approach to Marital Therapy. New York: Guilford.

———— (1970) Trick or Treatment: How and When Psychotherapy Fails. Champaign, IL: Research Press.

SULLIVAN, R. J. (1982) "Trends in automated human services." Social Work 27: 359-360.

SUNDEL, S. S. and M. SUNDEL (1980) Be Assertive: A Practical Guide for Human Service Workers. Beverly Hills, CA: Sage.

TALLENT, N. (1976) Psychological Report Writing. Englewood Cliffs, NJ: Prentice-Hall.

Temporary State Commission on Child Welfare (1976) The Children of the State: Barriers to the Freeing of Children for Adoption. New York: New York State Department of Social Services.

TOKARZ, T. and P. S. LAWRENCE (1974) "An analysis of temporal and stimulus factors in the treatment of insomnia." Presented at the meeting of the Association For Advancement of Behavior Therapy, Chicago, November.

TOWLE, C. (1954) Common Human Needs. Public Assistance Report 8. Washington, DC: Social Security Board.

TROPMAN, J. E. with B. MILLS (1980) Effective Meetings. Beverly Hills, CA: Sage.

TROWER, P., B. BRYANT, and M. ARGYLE (1978) Social Skills and Mental Health. London: Methuen.

TURNER, A. J. and W. H. GOODSON (1977) "Behavior technology applied to a community mental health center: a demonstration." Journal of Community Psychology 5: 209-224.

TURNER, A. J. and W. E. LEE (1976a) "Motivation through behavior modification, part 1: the job contract." Health Services Manager 9: 1-5.

———— (1976b) "Motivation through behavior modification, part 2: evaluation." Health Services Manager 9: 1-4.

U.S. Department of Health, Education and Welfare (1978) Child Abuse and Neglect Information Management Systems. Report from the Second National Conference on Data Aspects of Child Protective Services. DHEW Publication (OHDS) 79-30165. Washington, DC: Author.

WAHLER, R. G., G. H. WINKEL, R. F. PETERSON, and D. C. MORRISON (1965) "Mothers as behavior therapists for their own children." Behavior Research and Therapy 3: 113-134.

WALKER, C. E. Learn To Relax: 13 Ways To Reduce Tension. Englewood Cliffs NJ: Prentice-Hall.

WATSON, D. L. and R. G. THARP (1981) Self-Directed Behavior: Self-Modification for personal adjustment. Monterey, A: Brooks/Cole.

WEINER, B., I. FRIEZE, A. KUKLA, L. REED, S. REST, and R. M. ROSENBAUM (1971) "Perceiving the causes of success and failure," in E. E. Jones et al. (eds.)

Attribution: Perceiving the Causes of Behavior. Morristown, NJ: General Learning Press.

WEINRICH, T. W., F. S. PERLMUTTER, and W. C. RICHAN (1977) "Interorganizational behavior patterns of line staff and services integration." Social Services Review 51: 674-689.

WENAR, C., and J. B. COULTER (1962) "A reliability study of developmental histories." Child Development 33: 453-462.

WHITE, S. H., M. C. DAY, P. K. FREEMAN, S. A. HAUPTMAN, and K. T. MESSENGER (1973) Federal Programs for Young Children: Review and Recommendations, vol. 1. Washington, DC: Superintendent of Documents.

WOLINS, M. (1963) Selecting Foster Parents. New York: Columbia University Press.

YARROW, M. R., J. D. CAMPBELL, and R. V. BURTON (1970) "Recollections of childhood: a study of the retrospective method." Monographs of the Society for Research in Child Development 35, 5 (Serial No. 138).

ZANDER, A. (1982) Making Groups Effective. San Francisco: Jossey-Bass.

ABOUT THE AUTHORS

Eileen Gambrill is Professor of Social Welfare at the University of California at Berkeley. She has been involved in the area of child welfare since 1972. She was principal investigator of a training grant from the federal government to develop materials for child welfare supervisors. This resulted in the publication of *Supervision In Child Welfare: A Training Manual* (with T. Stein), on which the current book is based. Her publications include *Children In Foster Homes* (with Stein and Wiltse), *Casework: A Competency Based Approach*, and Resources on Foster Care and Adoption in Britain (in *Children and Youth Services Review*, 1981). Professor Gambrill (together with T. Stein) is guest editor of a special issue of *Children and Youth Service Review* on Permanency Planning.

Theodore J. Stein is Professor at the School of Social Work, New York University. He was project director of the Alameda Project, an experimental project comparing the effectiveness of systematic decision-making procedures, designed to increase continuity of care for children, with usual county procedures. Professor Stein just completed a three-year project evaluating the effectiveness of systematic procedures for making intake decisions in child welfare agencies. Recent books include *Children In Foster Homes: Achieving Continuity of Care* (with Gambrill and Wiltse); *Social Work Practice In Child Welfare*, and *Decision Making At Child Welfare Intake — A Handbook for Practitioners* (with Rzepnicki).

NOTES

NOTES

NOTES

NOTES